A YEAR OF POSITIVE THINKING

A YEAR OF
Positive
THINKING

DAILY INSPIRATION, WISDOM, AND COURAGE

CYNDIE SPIEGEL

ALTHEA
PRESS

For general information on our other products and services or to obtain technical support, please contact our Customer Care Department within the U.S. at (866) 744-2665, or outside the U.S. at (510) 253-0500.

Althea Press publishes its books in a variety of electronic and print formats. Some content that appears in print may not be available in electronic books, and vice versa.

TRADEMARKS: Althea Press and the Althea Press logo are trademarks or registered trademarks of Callisto Media Inc. and/or its affiliates, in the United States and other countries, and may not be used without written permission. All other trademarks are the property of their respective owners. Althea Press is not associated with any product or vendor mentioned in this book.

Interior Designer: Liz Cosgrove
Cover Designer: Amy King and Alyssa Nassner
Editor: Melissa Valentine
Production Editor: Andrew Yackira
Illustrations: Anugraha Design/Creative Market Labs Inc.
Author photo: © Ira James Photography, 2018.

ISBN: Print 978-1-64152-241-0 | eBook 978-1-64152-242-7

To my Mom:
Thank you for teaching me resilience,
fierce honesty, and unconditional love.
I am the woman I am because of you.

To my brothers:
You are worthy and you matter.
Thank you for teaching me what strength
and resilience truly are.

And of course to Ira:
Without you, I wouldn't have the words
to write this book. I love you.

Contents

Introduction

In some ways, I'm an unlikely candidate to write a book on positive thinking. I'm a realist, and I was not raised to view the world through rose-colored glasses.

My mom was a tough and protective, yet loving and softhearted, stay-at-home mother who had her first of four children at age 20 and had to raise us all largely on her own. My father was a hard-drinking, bighearted, blue-collar nomad until I was eight years old, when he finally moved into our home. We lived in a fairly poor neighborhood where there was little in the way of community support, and my three older brothers and I were troubled kids. We often learned life lessons the hard way—lessons like the world isn't always fair, but it is what it is. That we would do what we could with the cards we were dealt. That there's no use crying over spilled milk. And those things may absolutely be true.

As an adult, I've learned other valuable lessons that are equally true. I've learned that the world is filled with both abundance and scarcity, cruelty and kindness, despair and hope. I've learned that our lives are very similar to the segments and the peel of an orange; they are both bitter and sweet, and we can't experience one without having the other.

I have also learned that the ability to see light within the darkness creates a world of wide-open, heart-bursting possibility. I've learned that this perspective is a choice and that choosing positivity over negativity requires both clarity and courage. These lessons have come to me as I've immersed myself in practices, traditions, and fields that explore how we can affect our *mind-set*, including yoga, meditation, Buddhism, Hinduism, traditional academic education, and most notably, positive psychology.

Positive psychology has helped me cultivate a mind-set of positivity, grace, and abundance, allowing me to make them key parts of my everyday experience. It also reinforced the qualities of grit, resilience, and post-traumatic growth that I acquired early in my life. With this mind-set as my foundation, I was able to make a major career change in my mid-30s and then create multiple successful businesses. Today, the theories of positive psychology are what I practice and teach every day as a strategic business coach and transformational speaker. They are also the framework for positive thinking.

Here is the most empowering thing you should know as you begin reading this book: You can physically change your brain by consciously changing your thoughts. And you have the capacity to change your thoughts regardless of your race, socioeconomic background, or religious beliefs.

How exactly do your thoughts reshape your brain? Through neuroplasticity, the brain's ability to reorganize itself by forming new neural connections throughout our lives. Because new thoughts create new neural pathways and repeated thoughts reinforce existing ones, our thoughts can literally change the structure and the function of our brains. By using repetitive mental activities like positive thinking, we can retrain our brains to become more inclined toward positive feelings.

But focusing on the positive can be a challenge, because of our brain's *negativity bias*; essentially our brains are neurologically wired to look for what is wrong instead of what is going well. Negativity bias is the reason negative experiences weigh much heavier on our minds than positive ones of the same intensity.

Barbara L. Fredrickson, PhD, a well-known scholar of positive psychology and author of the book *Positivity*, says that it takes approximately three positive thoughts to outweigh just one negative thought. Visualize a balance scale—one of those that has a horizontal crosspiece with a weighing pan hanging from each arm. In one pan are feathers; in the other are pebbles. The feathers are positive thoughts, and pebbles are negative ones. To get the scale to tip toward the feather side, we need three feathers for every one pebble. We need *a lot* of positive thoughts to counteract the negative thoughts that are affecting our brain.

So, when you decide to exercise your ability to consciously engage positive thoughts, you are engaging in some powerful, mind-shifting magic. And when you change how you think, you change how you act and who you are in the world.

I've compiled this book of wisdom, courage, and inspiration so that you can experience the power of positive thinking and positive psychology for yourself, in quick and easy ways. By reading just one entry in this book each day, you can steadily shift your mind-set from one that clings to every negative experience, to one that embraces hope, encouragement, bravery, resilience, and possibility.

My wish for you is that, as you turn each page, you become more empowered to show up in your life with positivity, grace, and courage. And for those days when you can't, my wish is that this book will comfort you until you are once again ready to experience the world through the lens of forgiveness, resilience, and love.

I hope that you find in this book the words you need to heal, live, love, thrive, and courageously be whoever you are meant to be in this wild, crazy world. As you read these pages, my hope is that you feel redeemed in your humanity and that you feel more understood—not only because of your strengths, but also because of the strength that you inhabit within your perceived weaknesses.

If you're ready—*really* ready—to live your best life, then let's begin, shall we?

JANUARY

RIGHT WHERE YOU SHOULD BE

You are in exactly the right place.

That place may be scary, boring, exciting, or heartbreaking. But whatever it is, *sit tight*. Instead of fighting your way out of it with everything you've got, sit still.

Experience it.
Let go.
Rock on.
You are exactly where you should be.

THE WISDOM OF *KINTSUKUROI*

Kintsukuroi is a kind of Japanese ceramic style. The word Kintsukuroi means "to repair with gold." In the Kintsukuroi tradition, when a ceramic piece breaks, an artisan will fuse the pieces back together using liquid gold or gold-dusted lacquer. So rather than being covered up, the breaks become more obvious, and a new piece of art emerges from the brokenness.

Kintsukuroi embraces flaws and imperfection, but it also teaches the essence of resilience. Every crack in a ceramic piece is part of its history, and each piece becomes more beautiful because it has been broken.

> You will fall.
> You will fail.
> You will break.
> You will stand up and dust yourself off.
> You will repair yourself again and again.
> And eventually, though you will be different than before, you will again become whole.
> You will be even more beautiful precisely because of all of this.
> You will be a better person because of your imperfections, not in spite of them.

TAKE THE INITIATIVE

"Don't wait around for other people to be happy for you. Any happiness you get you've got to make yourself."

—ALICE WALKER

4

JANUARY

THE WISDOM OF IMPERMANENCE

Every experience that you have is simply *one moment* in time. Every moment that you struggle within, sit with, or dance your way through will eventually pass.

This truth applies to all things—the good and the difficult, the darkness and the light, the just and the unjust. It is all transient, momentary.

There is both grace and wisdom in knowing that this moment, too, will eventually pass.

5

JANUARY

CREATE YOUR OWN SUNSHINE

If you want happiness, choose it. Don't wait for anyone to bestow it upon you. Live your life like you mean it, damn it. This is all there is. Appreciate the nuance of who you are. Find wonder in your surroundings. Notice the rainbows after the rain. And when rain gets you down, create your own sunshine because you are the only one who can.

6

JANUARY

DON'T GIVE YOUR THOUGHTS TOO MUCH POWER

Your thoughts are subjective and flexible, so don't allow them to rule every choice that you make. Just like you think negative thoughts, you can think more positive ones, too. You can train yourself to think differently by acting in ways that align with the thoughts you'd prefer to have and catching yourself when you have thoughts that don't align. Changing your thinking is a practice, but one well worth the time. Considering that you have between 50,000 and 70,000 thoughts per day, it pays not to give your thoughts too much power over your life.

7

JANUARY

EXPECTATION: THE THIEF OF JOY

Be careful of expectations that you set for others, but more importantly, be careful of the ones you set for yourself. Expectation rarely leaves room for the wonder and magic of the unknown.

8

JANUARY

~

YOU ARE COMPLETELY RESPONSIBLE FOR YOUR LIFE

This truth is equal parts empowering and terrifying. It means that you have to consciously let go of blame, misunderstandings, and excuses that don't support you. Though it doesn't justify any wrongdoing that you've experienced, it does give you the power to change what makes you unhappy. By accepting responsibility for where you are right now, regardless of how you got here, you are better positioned to change the way your story plays out.

9

JANUARY

~

YOU WILL MAKE MISTAKES

You will make mistakes because you're human, but how you learn from them is solely up to you. There will be times when you get it wrong, and your ego will feel the sting. But trust that you don't have to know everything or have all the right answers. You will learn what you need to when you need to. To move forward with grace and humility, be open to the opinions of others and to learning from your mistakes.

〜

BELIEVE

....

be·lieve \ bə-lēv \ verb

1. Accept (something) as true; feel sure of the truth of.

....

You unconsciously create experiences that match what you believe about yourself and others. So ask yourself these questions often: "What do I believe about myself and my life? Is what I believe truly serving who I want to be in the world?"

Be mindful of what you accept as truth. Because you become what you believe, for better or worse.

11
JANUARY

IN GOOD COMPANY

Spend time in the company of those who can stand up for you when you are unable, those who believe in you when you are unwilling, those who honor the magnitude of your greatness, even when you are not quite ready to yourself.

They see you for who you are. Trust them, show them love, and honor these relationships.

12
JANUARY

KINDNESS

When someone says something kind about you, choose to believe them.

YOU WILL FIND EXACTLY WHAT YOU EXPECT

When I question my own perspective, this anecdote, shared by one of my teachers, reminds me to be more mindful of my thoughts:

A woman walked up to a gate of a guarded community and asked, "What kind of people are here in your community?"

The man at the gate replied, "What kind of people are there where you are from?"

"Well, they are mean, rude, nasty, and shortsighted," she said.

"You will find the same people here," he told her.

A few minutes later, another woman walked up to the man and asked, "What kind of people are here in this community?"

The man at the gate replied, "What kind of people are there where you are from?"

"They are kind, loving, authentic, and good," she said.

"You will find the same people here," he told her.

And so it is. We often find exactly what we believe we will.

14

JANUARY

IT DOES GET BETTER

You will experience moments when you feel like the world is against you, when nothing seems to work, when it feels like everything that can go wrong has.

There are some circumstances that can't be fixed or made better immediately. There will be times when your world does not feel okay.

As best as possible, you must sit and honor this truth.

In those moments, allow yourself to cry, shout, or be upset. Feel what you feel. But then surrender into what is.

I can't say when or how, but time, surrender, and healing will allow you to find solace.

It does get better. Know this.

15
JANUARY

SHOW UP AND SPEAK UP

Show up in the world in a way that makes you proud. Speak words that you wouldn't be ashamed to hear repeated back to you.

16
JANUARY

YOU CAN BEGIN AGAIN

There will be times when you've come as far as you can, when your heart is broken open and you see no way through.

When those moments present themselves to you, sit quietly, courageously feel what you feel, and then, and only then, let go—as gracefully as you can.

Grace is knowing for certain that you will inevitably be hurt again and knowing just as certainly that you are strong, you are resilient, and all of it will make you more beautiful.

It is only through our brokenness that our light can shine.

You will begin again.

17

JANIARY

IT'S OKAY TO SAY NO

"No."

"Nope."

"Not now."

"Not going to happen."

"Possibly not ever."

Now is as good a time as any to stop saying yes to things you really want to say no to. If you've been waiting for permission to say no, permission granted. Say yes to the things you choose and no to the things you don't.

18

JANUARY

LIGHT IT UP

You can light up your own damn life. Stop waiting for someone else to do it for you.

19
JANUARY

GOOD SURPRISES

Life will surprise you in the most magnificent ways. Allow it to.
Be on the lookout for wonder, generosity, and unexpected smiles.
Graciously accept them when they show up.

20
JANUARY

WORTHINESS IS A CHOICE

You are worthy—more worthy than you will ever understand. But the only
one who can ultimately determine that reality is you.

21
JANUARY

~

THE CAPACITY TO FORGIVE

"We must develop and maintain the capacity to forgive. He who is devoid of the power to forgive is devoid of the power to love ... There is some good in the worst of us and some evil in the best of us. When we discover this, we are less prone to hate our enemies."

—MARTIN LUTHER KING JR.

22

JANUARY

HAPPINESS ISN'T OUT THERE

Happiness isn't found out on a beach somewhere basking in the hot sun. It isn't found in a cocktail glass or in approval from others. It is not something you need to chase or find.

Instead, you can create it right here, where you are now, with the choices you make each day.

Choose to take good care of yourself. Do what brings you joy. Live a life you believe in. Spend time in the company of those who uplift you. Be kind.

Happiness is the side effect of all of these experiences; it is not a thing you find *out there*.

WORDS TO LIVE BY

Be kind—often.

Life isn't always easy, and you have no idea what other folks are experiencing.

Your truth is yours. Leave space for someone else's, too.

Trust in people.

Believe in what you can't see.

Know that the world is an inherently beautiful place.

Believe that you are exactly as you're supposed to be.

Trust your journey.

Be a force for good shit.

And for the love of all things holy, be kind.

HOW YOU PERCEIVE THE WORLD IS HOW YOU WILL LIVE

You can choose to focus on each awful, imperfect experience. You can assume the worst possible outcome and expect people to fail you.

Or you can allow yourself to be in awe of what is right, beautiful, sacred, and profound. You can choose to focus on what makes you feel aligned with the extraordinary life you hope for. You can expect people to surprise and delight you in the best possible ways.

What you focus on is what will become your truth. Choose wisely.

25

JANUARY

~

TRUE EMPATHY

Be wide open to the plight of others unlike yourself. By feeling the range of the ups and downs of humanity, you crack open your spirit to allow in empathy—but not the kind of empathy that breaks you apart in so many pieces that you can't get up. That is not empathy, but sympathy, pity, shame, or fear masquerading as empathy. True empathy allows you to envelop yourself in the truth of others in a way that makes the world a kinder, gentler place.

In this kind of empathy, you find the truest form of grace.

26

JANUARY

~

KARMA

"How people treat you is their karma, how you react is yours."

—WAYNE W. DYER

27

JANUARY

~

A LIFE OF YOUR OWN CHOOSING

What would you do differently if the opinions of others didn't matter?

Write a list. Prioritize the items in order of what you are most excited about.

Start doing all of the things on your list. Then, consciously enjoy living a life of your own choosing.

28

JANUARY

~

LIVE LIFE WITH ABANDON

This one life is all you've got. So, above all else, live it with unbridled abandon and openhearted curiosity. Be brave. Allow creativity to be your guide. Live as if no one else were watching. Dance. Play. Sing out loud. Make the kind of magic that dreams are built of.

29

JANUARY

APOLOGIES AND ASKING FOR FORGIVENESS ARE NOT THE SAME

Saying "I'm sorry" doesn't make you free of guilt. And forgiveness doesn't mean that harm has not been done.

An apology simply means that you are sorry for a transgression. But asking for forgiveness shows that your relationship is more important than your ego and that your hope is to recover the respect that may have been lost because of that transgression.

Acknowledgment of wrongdoing is powerful, but the humility demonstrated in asking for forgiveness is when you courageously evoke your greatest strength.

BE DONE EACH DAY

"Finish each day and be done with it. You have done what you could. Some blunders and absurdities no doubt crept in; forget them as soon as you can. Tomorrow is a new day. You shall begin it serenely and with too high a spirit to be encumbered with your old nonsense."

—RALPH WALDO EMERSON

THE PRACTICE OF GRATITUDE

Gratitude shapes how you experience life.

It's easy to be grateful when everything goes as planned. But if you can be grateful even when the shit hits the fan, then you will feel the most profound impact of gratitude. Gratitude doesn't take away pain or sadness, but it does allow you to shift your focus toward what you can control.

Being grateful is a practice, and like any practice, it gets deeper and richer with commitment and discipline. Having a committed daily gratitude practice will make you happier and a whole lot more empathetic.

What are you grateful for right now? Write down three positive experiences that you've had today. Challenge yourself to write a short gratitude list every night for the next 10 days.

At the end of the 10 days, share your gratitude lists with three people close to you. Notice the impact that this extended practice has on your life.

FEBRUARY

1
FEBRUARY

~~~

YOU ARE THE ONE YOU ARE WAITING FOR

Love begins with you.

There is no one who can make you more whole than you already are, even in your perceived brokenness. You cannot expect others to be perfect, and you cannot expect yourself to be perfect, either. If the love of another is what you seek, it's damn near impossible to ask someone else to give you what you are unable to give yourself first.

You are the one you've been waiting for. The love you hope for begins with you; it always has.

How do you love yourself? What parts of yourself perhaps need more love from you? What can you do as a part of a daily routine to maintain a loving relationship with yourself?

MANIFESTO FOR A LIFE WELL LIVED

Do what you believe in. Trust your intuition.
Do something kind for someone else every day.
Dance alone at least once a week.
Cry and feel whatever you feel.
Laugh riotously and often—the kind of laughter that makes your
    belly hurt.
Do the weird things that only you understand.
Love yourself as you are.
Love others as they are. (You can't change people anyway.)
Dance to your own beat, even when no one else hears the music.
The acceptance you've been waiting for only emerges when you
    allow yourself to be completely, unabashedly you.

3

FEBRUARY

LESSONS ON LOVE

1. Sometimes the one you think is right is all kinds of wrong *for you.*

2. There are a lot of folks with low expectations of what's possible in matters of the heart. Remember, you get exactly what you allow yourself to receive.

3. You will, without question, experience the kind of love that cracks your heart wide open and sprinkles confetti on the table—but not until you decide that nothing less than this is an option.

4. Love is compromise, but if you find yourself in a relationship where the prerequisite is change, for either you or your partner, walk away and save yourself the heartbreak.

5. All matters of the heart have challenges, but the lay-your-soul-on-the-line kind of love is one of the most natural feelings in the world.

6. When you unconditionally love someone, you see them as they are. When you love them with condition, you see them as you are.

7. Love is wide-open freedom in a tightly confined world.

8. When it's right, you feel it in every cell of your being. When it's wrong, you feel that, too. Stay in close connection to your heart to know what is true for you.

9. Cynicism has a way of settling in, and if you allow it to, you can easily give up faith in the one thing that can save us all: love. Please don't lose your faith. Love does exist.

10. Most importantly, you deserve to be loved. You deserve to be loved. You deserve to be loved.

CHOOSE KINDNESS OVER RIGHTEOUSNESS

The need to be right is an unfortunately common feeling in the human experience.

The ego wants to be right. The heart wants to be kind. Act from the heart and choose kindness. There is strength in the willingness to gently surrender.

When you find yourself face to face in a disagreement, ask yourself these simple questions: "Is being right really going to serve me in this moment? Will it fix anything? How can I instead listen with kindness and gently surrender?" You may surprise yourself with your ability to choose graciously.

BREATHE, LET GO

"So stop and take a look at your own needs. Go mindless. Let go. And remind yourself that this very moment is the only one you know you have for sure."

—OPRAH WINFREY, *WHAT I KNOW FOR SURE*

FEBRUARY

APPRECIATE THE MOMENT

For every day that you wake, be unbelievably grateful, because somewhere there is someone else who will not.

For every moment that you concern yourself with the goings-on of others, keep in mind that they too have problems.

For every second that you doubt the authenticity of your loving relationships, consider that many people are alone.

For each moment that you question your own worthiness, realize that you are the exact amount of enough.

Appreciate the beauty in everything, knowing that one day it will be long gone.

FEBRUARY

A BROKEN HEART AND SHINING LIGHT

Inevitably, your heart will break into a million pieces—possibly more than once. But you will be okay. You will experience loss, grief, heartache, and, eventually, solace.

But first, allow yourself to feel the full scope of what you feel. You don't want to hide behind a hardened heart and a darkened soul forever.

When you decide to surrender, you will let in the sunlight.

And once you do, you will reflect that light back into your heart and then out into the world.

FEBRUARY

WORDS MATTER

The words you use determine the world you inhabit. If you say you can't, you won't. If you assume you can, you will.

Be deliberate with your language, because what you say often becomes your truth. And your truth becomes your life.

9

FEBRUARY

BE LOVE

Show love.
Give love.
Manifest love.
Teach love.
Be love.

10
FEBRUARY

YOUR LOVE MATTERS

Love comes in whatever form you need it most. And all forms are equally valid and valuable.

Write your own story of love, and know that you don't ever have to follow the script that someone else assigned you. Love whomever you love. Love however you love. But always choose love.

11
FEBRUARY

THE WORLD DOESN'T NEED MORE SAMENESS

Say what you feel. Wear what you want. Do what you please. Believe what you believe. Have your opinion.

Graciously hear the opinions of others, but do not allow anyone to bully you out of your truth.

Stand in who you are. Take a stand for others.

Celebrate what makes you different. The world is awaiting your honest, rebellious, and wild soul. Show us who you truly are.

12
FEBRUARY

THE FAMILY YOU CHOOSE

Your community is the family you get to choose. Choose wisely; connect with others consciously.

Some friendships will grow and shift along with you, while others will dissolve as you evolve. Try not to take this personally; it doesn't make the relationship any less valuable. Faithfully honor the friends that grow with you. Cherish them. Consider yourself one of the lucky ones to have such long friendships. And when time allows, welcome new friendships with curiosity, love, and a wide-open heart. These new friends, too, can become a part of your beautifully curated family.

13
FEBRUARY

~~~

TODAY ONLY

"Don't let yesterday take up too much of today."

—WILL ROGERS

14
FEBRUARY

~~~

COURAGE AND BRAVERY

Courage is the willful strength to fight and the mindfulness to understand why you're fighting. Bravery is the strength of character that allows you to overcome.

Be courageous enough to hold onto the fights that you need to, but also brave enough to let go of what is not worth fighting for.

15
FEBRUARY

A RITUAL FOR LOVE

There is great audacity in allowing yourself to love and be loved by another person, imperfections and all. Here is a simple weekly ritual for love.

Light a red or pink candle.
Sit quietly, with your feet flat on the ground and your
    spine upright, or lay down fully.
Read the words below, repeating them as many times
    as you'd like.

May I choose love and allow myself to be seen.
May I allow love to break my soul open and dwell
    in my heart.
May I allow others to love me and return that
    love wholeheartedly.
May I be love—joyful, discerning, and unwavering.
May I always courageously choose love in whichever
    way fulfills me.

Then, allow all kinds of love to pour in.

16
FEBRUARY

~

BECOME AN EXPERT IN YOU

There is no one else as good at being you than you are. Be open to receiving advice but also trust that you know yourself better than anyone. You are an expert in your own experiences; own that. Boldly accept what makes you different. Believe in your abilities. Trust your intuition. Stand up for your ideas, and know that you are exactly who you should be.

17
FEBRUARY

~

FRIENDSHIP AS SOUL MATES

We often seek lovers to connect at a soul level, but good friends can be soul mates, too.

How can you tell if a friend is a soul mate? They don't simply tolerate your imperfections; they love you because of them. Home is wherever they are, whether you're both silent for hours or talking loudly into the evening with a bottle of wine or a hot cup of tea. In this great big world, when you've found a person whose crazy matches yours, and your life has become brighter because of it, if that's not a soul mate, then I don't know what is.

DIVERSITY IS BEAUTY

"We need to give each other the space to grow, to be ourselves, to exercise our diversity. We need to give each other space so that we may both give and receive such beautiful things as ideas, openness, dignity, joy, healing, and inclusion."

—MAX DE PREE, *LEADERSHIP IS AN ART*

SURROUND YOURSELF WITH PEOPLE
WHO SPEAK TRUTH TO YOUR BULLSHIT

You need people in your life who are kind, accepting, and loving, but it is equally important to have people who "speak truth to bullshit," as professor Brené Brown, PhD, often says.

Our friends are our compasses: they show us the way and redirect us when we've settled too low or our pride is leading us away from our center. Our ego often gets in the way of true friendship because we feign the good stuff, the things that allow us to simply get by in life without having to work too much. We don't always want to be challenged because truth-telling and honesty can hurt. The true power of good friends is that they will respect the fragility of our hearts, but also require us to step into our own truth with grace and honesty.

Surround yourself with people who uplift you, but who also speak truth to your bullshit.

THE WINDY ROAD UPWARD

It's easy to look at what others have achieved and measure your own success or progress against it.

But no one starts out at "the top," and no one gets there the same way. One of the most courageous things you'll ever do is trust that there is, in fact, a path—and that path is whichever windy road you are traveling. Your path won't always be straight, and it won't always be easy. But it will always be yours, and it will always lead you to the mountaintop that is perfect for you. Trust that.

21
FEBRUARY

THE COURAGE OF KINDNESS

Kindness is the willingness to support and celebrate others in a world where selfishness is often the default. One of the most underrated qualities of kindness is the courage that it takes to stand for someone other than yourself. Having the generosity of spirit to recognize the obstacles of others and support them—*that takes courage.* And that kind of courage inspires kindness in others and creates a ripple effect in all of us.

22
FEBRUARY

YOU DON'T NEED APPROVAL

Don't concern yourself with what others think of your choices. Instead, firmly stand for them. Your decisions are your own. You choose how you show up in the world and who you spend your time with. Do whatever brings you to your knees with joy, gratitude, and belonging, and do not seek approval from others. Know that what is right for you may not be right for someone else, and that's okay. Stand in all that you choose—with no approval needed.

GRATITUDE AND PERFECTION

Some days, you feel like you've failed at life because you haven't done it perfectly. You said the thing you shouldn't have, or you didn't do the one thing you should have.

When that happens, consider this instead:

You are human, and you're figuring out life with as much resilience and grace as you can muster. You made it to another day because you are supposed to be here.

And in the moments when the weight of your perceived imperfection feels especially heavy, practice gratitude. Say thank you for what you've done right. That graciousness will shift everything, because gratitude is reciprocal. Bestow it on yourself always, but especially when you need it most.

REALITY AND DREAMS COEXIST IN POSSIBILITY

Dreams exist to lead us toward new possibilities. Dreams are not in competition with reality. You can have both. Your version of being realistic doesn't mean that you can't work toward a bigger, brighter, and more bold vision. But the moment that you decide that you must choose one or the other, you've chosen fear over possibility. You've chosen your current experience over what could be.

Consider that reality is simply what you make it. And you get to decide what your reality is.

The world can sometimes be too cynical; don't allow that cynicism to creep into your vision of what's possible. And don't allow someone else's version of reality to compromise your dreams.

~~~

EVERY SINGLE MOMENT MATTERS

Every moment matters—not just the big ones, but also the small ones, the seemingly irrelevant ones and the quiet ones. All of these moments add up to a life well lived.

Don't take the presumably unimportant moments for granted. Look for them and treasure them instead. Listen for the words unspoken. Notice the quick glance. Feel the soft touch. The long-held hugs. The sadness. The graciousness. The in-between.

The magical sweet spots between tiny and massive moments are your life. Don't forget to pay attention to them. In the end, this is really all we have.

26
FEBRUARY

~

"A thousand-mile journey begins with a single step."

—LAO TZU, *TAO TE CHING*

Rome wasn't built in a day, and neither is your ideal life.

First you have to begin—exactly where you are.

Then, one step leads to another, which leads to another. Know that sometimes there may be two steps forward and five steps back.

Be patient with yourself. Take your time. Walk slowly. And trust that with each step you are making progress on your "thousand-mile journey," whatever it may be for you.

THINGS DO GET BETTER

When you are in the midst of the rubbish that life sometimes tosses your way, it feels impossible to gain perspective.

When those moments come, hold tight. Things will get better.

But first, be willing to work through whatever you are experiencing. No running, no distractions, and no negotiation.

Sit still, quiet down, and listen inward.

What is your experience telling you? What is needed? What can be learned?

This is the hard part. But you can do it—and you will.

Eventually, you will end up on the other side with a resilience that you didn't know you had.

28

FEBRUARY

THE THING ABOUT PERFECTION

It's easy to think that other people's lives are perfect compared to ours. But the perfection we think we are seeing is usually no more than a façade. It's like the exterior of a building that takes a whole lot of effort and good lighting to maintain. The inside of the building isn't usually as pristine, and it's certainly not perfect.

What might happen if you stopped censoring your life to achieve perfection? Who would you be if, instead of striving to present a perfect you to the world, you allowed the world to see who you really are inside?

MARCH

1
MARCH

STAND-DOWN MOMENTS

"We all have stand-down moments that require us to stand up, in the center of ourselves, and know who we are. When your marriage falls apart, when the job that defined you is gone, when the people you'd counted on turn their backs on you, there's no question that changing the way you think about your situation is the key to improving it. I know for sure that all of our hurdles have meaning. And being open to learning from challenges is the difference between succeeding and getting stuck."

—OPRAH WINFREY, *WHAT I KNOW FOR SURE*

2
MARCH

~~~

CULTIVATE HOPE

Cultivate hope above all else. Allow it to permeate your life and seep into your heart.

There will be times when you are on top of the world and others where you find yourself in a heap of tears.

Both are necessary. But without hope, nothing else is possible.

What gives you hope? Who gives you hope? These become your resources and when the world around you seems too dark to bear they become your beacon of light and your reminder of hope.

3
MARCH

~~~

CYNICISM

Cynicism is easy: it is simply judgment and fear.

Choose curiosity instead.

4
MARCH

DISENTANGLE FROM THE PAST

Disentangle yourself from the past to embrace the future. Don't reside in your childhood, regardless of how wonderful or imperfect it was. Move forward with all of the grace and acceptance you can muster.

Let go. Love boldly. Grow. Learn.

Then, spread your wings and soar.

5
MARCH

SHINE BRIGHT

When you wake up every day, remind yourself that whoever you are is a choice.

You create the narrative, so don't be afraid to highlight your humor, brilliance, and bravery. You are not here to be small.

Come to terms with that truth, then sit back and brace yourself for the beauty that is you.

Allow your light to shine brightly; there is never enough of your luminescence in this sometimes darkened world.

6
MARCH

ADVERSITY

Adversity is one of the greatest growth opportunities you can receive. It will teach you how to fall apart and come back together. It will show you how to hope, believe, and dream. It prepares you to soar to unbelievable heights.

Journeying through adversity teaches you how to move beyond survival and into thriving. It demonstrates that love and persistence are your birthright.

That journey is your gift, and your job is to share that gift with others.

It grants you the ability to shine your light outward for the world to receive.

7
MARCH

CHOOSE KINDNESS

Always choose kindness.
The world has enough assholes.

8
MARCH

YOU DESERVE TO BE HEARD

Your voice is your power. Speak your truth clearly and with great compassion. You deserve to be heard, so take a stand for yourself. Boldly stay the course, and confidently stand up tall. When you are ready to speak, the world will listen. Trust that your words will resonate with those who need to hear them most.

9
MARCH

LIGHTNESS

Try not to be so damn precious with yourself. You are doing the best you can. Show yourself the same grace that you would offer others. Know that everything that needs to happen will. Take solace in that wisdom. You are not in control of the universe, but you do have a choice in how you show up in your life. Ease up. Allow in lightness. Forgive yourself.

Go on, grant yourself permission to live a life that makes you more joyful than you ever imagined possible.

10
MARCH

~~~

LONELINESS

Although the world is beautiful and vast, it can also sometimes be bitter, and in those moments, we can experience great loneliness within. Know that you are never alone when feeling lonely. Give yourself permission to nourish community, seek out friendships, and joyously cultivate love. Don't be afraid to speak to strangers; they may become friends. Let diversity and curiosity overcome fear; we are more alike than we are different.

Stand in love instead of indifference, and become a beacon of kindness for others who are experiencing their own loneliness.

11
MARCH

~~~

CHOOSE HAPPY

Let this be a kind reminder that you—and only you—are the gatekeeper of your own happiness. Delight in that wisdom.

12
MARCH

~~~

TODAY IS ALL THERE IS

Today is all there is. Live boldly. Forgive often. Love openly.

Give thanks for every beautiful experience. But also show gratitude for the ones that were difficult yet shined a light to show you the way forward.

Honor your own story—whatever it may be—with love, courage, and dignity. Do not strive for perfection, because, as you are, you exemplify the beauty of humanity in all of its imperfection and magnificence.

Today is all you have. So, with the full recognition of that immense, empowering truth, be present in this moment and honor it.

13
MARCH

~~~

YOUR PERCEPTION IS YOUR REALITY

Your perception becomes your reality. When you assume positivity, it is often what you discover. If you assume negativity, that, too, is what you'll find.

14
MARCH

~

WE DON'T FORGET HOW WE FEEL

"I've learned that people will forget what you said, people will forget what you did, but people will never forget how you made them feel."

—MAYA ANGELOU

15
MARCH

~

ORDINARY YOU ARE NOT

You are a unicorn in an ordinary world. This simple truth requires an acceptance that you will not please everyone. Be okay with this. Do not fear your own greatness. Surround yourself with people who appreciate your magic. Stand tall, shoulders back, and confidently speak your truth. Avoid trying to win the approval of others. And for the love of all things, don't ever allow yourself to play small to satisfy the needs of someone who cannot stand in your light.

16
MARCH

LISTEN WITH AN OPEN HEART

Be brave in the face of ignorance, but avoid quieting the opinions of others without listening first. We all want to be heard in a noisy world. Speak your truth boldly, but also try to understand the reasoning of others. You may not agree, but keep an open heart. Be willing to be wrong. The ability to empathetically listen to others may just be the one thing that saves us all. Trust that people are not inherently bad. Believe in the impossible. Know that people, like seasons, can change.

17
MARCH

YOUR PAST HAS BROUGHT YOU TO YOUR PRESENT

Make peace with your past: it showed you who you are. Every experience you've had before this moment created the beauty that is you. Accept that. Love yourself for all that you've become, but don't ever forget who you once were. Our most powerful lessons are garnered from our most difficult struggles.

18
MARCH

ON RECEIVING ADVICE

Many well-intentioned folks will advise you on how you should live your life. The choices they tell you to make might be right for them, but it doesn't mean they are right for you.

Assume that their intention is positive. Graciously say thank you. And then consciously choose to do whatever the hell you want to.

19
MARCH

AN EXERCISE IN ALIGNMENT

Listen closely for the call of your soul.

In which areas are you out of alignment with what you hope for? What things are you doing that don't feed your soul? Where is your focus being misused?

Acknowledge where you aren't listening to your soul. Give that misalignment room to exist. Then, create an exit plan that brings you back into alignment with your heart because this is the place where your genuine truth resides.

20
MARCH

DON'T BE AFRAID TO STAND OUT

There will always be a certain expectation of those who do things differently. Different is often misunderstood, but don't be afraid of that. That divergence is where glory resides. Graciously learn from others, but don't become them. Unless you've built the box, don't try to squeeze into it: it wasn't made to fit you. Allow your wild spirit to boldly flourish. Don't waste your magic by trying to be just like everyone else.

21
MARCH

POWER OVER HELPLESSNESS

A moment of weakness doesn't make you helpless. Shit happens to all of us. Stand up, dust off, and root down. Do not bemoan what you aren't capable of, but, instead, attempt what you believe is impossible. You are brilliant and gifted.

Yes, you will stumble and fall, but each time you rise again, you become more confident and capable. Powerlessness can easily become your narrative; do not allow it to. You are much stronger than you know.

22
MARCH

~

YOU'RE THE ONE IN CHARGE

"I have come to the frightening conclusion that I am the decisive element. It is my personal approach that creates the climate. It is my daily mood that makes the weather. I possess tremendous power to make life miserable or joyous. I can be a tool of torture or an instrument of inspiration, I can humiliate or humor, hurt or heal. In all situations, it is my response that decides whether a crisis is escalated or de-escalated, and a person is humanized or de-humanized. If we treat people as they are, we make them worse. If we treat people as they ought to be, we help them become what they are capable of becoming."

—JOHANN WOLFGANG VON GOETHE

23

MARCH

DO NOT DEFINE YOURSELF BY YOUR BEST OR YOUR WORST

The worst and the greatest of times do not define who you are. You will have bad days and better days. There will be days that are so brilliant that they bring you to your knees in grace.

But you are steadfast.

The compilation of all of your experiences is what makes you the marvelous human being that you've become. Avoid getting caught up in the extremes, because they, like all things, are ever-fleeting.

24

MARCH

WHAT FALLS MAY ALSO RISE

"You can fall, but you can rise also."

—ANGÉLIQUE KIDJO

25
MARCH

TAKE THE RISK

There is always a risk when you commit to authentically being who you are. You will be judged, and some people may not like you. As scary as that may seem, don't allow yourself to become complacent in an effort to be liked by everyone else. You will be judged anyway, so why not be judged based on who you truly are?

26
MARCH

DREAMS DEFERRED

Giving yourself the permission to dream takes courage. It is simpler to just accept what you're given.

To dream the impossible dream is scary. You could set expectations you may fail to meet. Things you hoped for may not turn out.

You may regret what happens. All of these are very real possible outcomes.

Alternatively, you may just receive everything you had the courage to dream up.

27
MARCH

~~~

YOU TEACH OTHERS HOW TO TREAT YOU

If you treat yourself with compassion and love, so, too, will others treat you. If you treat yourself with contempt and unkindness, you give others permission to do the same.

Define boundaries around your truth. Be willing to say no. Trust your intuition to guide your choices. Believe, without question, that you are deserving of respect and generosity. In so doing, you teach yourself and others to treat you with the love, kindness, and compassion that you are worthy of.

28
MARCH

~~~

ALWAYS CHOOSE LOVE

It's okay to be selective with your heart, but don't ever close yourself off to beautiful possibility. Choose courageously. Then, surrender and trust in what you know to be true. Love is a mutual dance that can realign the stars. Don't ever give up on it.

Love boldly, sweets. You are worthy of great love.

29
MARCH

THE WORLD WILL ALWAYS FALL BACK INTO PLACE

There will be days that set your soul on fire with triumph. There will be moments of such divine goodness that you dance in the streets in praise. Honor these times for the genuine magic that they are. With your heart wide open, graciously accept these moments.

But know that some days will be different. Do not judge yourself for the quiet times, the less confident days, and the sometimes somber nights. Those times, too, are necessary in an often too loud world.

Cry when you need to. Laugh when you are called to. Dance when you want to. Feel whatever you are compelled to.

Trust that the world will always fall back into place.

30
MARCH

DARE TO BE POWERFUL

"When I dare to be powerful, to use my strength in the service of my vision, then it becomes less and less important whether I am afraid."

—AUDRE LORDE, *THE CANCER JOURNALS*

AN EXERCISE FOR GRATITUDE

Instead of focusing on what you don't have, consider what you do have. Pull out a piece of paper and write a gratitude list.

Start with this simple prompt: "I am grateful for . . ."

Do not judge your list or criticize your entries. Simply write whatever comes to mind. Write until you've exhausted everything you can think of, big and small.

When you're done, tape your list to a prominent wall. Share it with the people you love. Take a picture of it and save it as the background on your phone or computer.

Watch your list grow.

Focusing on what you already have creates the space to bring even more into your life.

Remember, what you choose to focus on is what grows.

APRIL

1

~~~

THIS IS HAPPINESS

How would you recognize happiness unless you knew what unhappiness felt like? It's hard to have one without the other.

2

~~~

HOW TO OVERCOME

You overcome by accepting that there is no alternative except to pick yourself up, dust off, and continue moving forward. You don't give up or give in, even on the days you want to, because you know your life matters.

Overcoming adversity is what makes you resilient, and resiliency is what allows you to wake up each day with a sense of purpose, regardless of what you are experiencing. It teaches you that the fragility of your experience is not a curse, and it offers a greater vision of renewed possibility.

3
APRIL

YOU ARE

It takes courage to be your true self, vulnerability to allow others to see you, and wisdom to know that, regardless of what life tosses your way, you are enough.

You are courageous. You are vulnerable. You are wise. You are enough.

4
APRIL

AN EXERCISE IN "WHAT IF...?"

What if you stopped looking for others to be benchmarks for your own happiness?

What if you considered yourself a visionary, dreamer, a hero?

What if, just for today, you knew you were worthy of all that you wanted?

What would happen if you stopped comparing yourself to others and became your own measure for success? Who would you be in the world if you believed that to be true?

Perhaps, just for today, become that person.

I'M SORRY, FRIEND.

I'm sorry.

I'm sorry.

I'm sorry.

For whatever happened to you that made you feel less than, I am sorry.

You don't deserve that.

Sometimes there is no other answer. And in those moments, a tiny bit of empathy and a lot of love go a very long way.

Don't forget to say "I'm sorry" to yourself, too—as much as you need to.

The greatest forgiveness is the forgiveness you show yourself.

6

APRIL

~~~

DON'T MAKE IT HARDER THAN IT IS

Don't choose to make life harder than it is. Rather than getting caught up in the moment, consider the situation that you are annoyed, angry, or frustrated by.

Is it really worth having a bad day? Could you choose differently? Could you choose to be happy, regardless? Could you simply let it go and keep going? What might happen if you do?

Perspective is a gift, especially in moments of challenge.

7

APRIL

~~~

CONTINUE TO THRIVE

The world isn't always fair; time has a keen way of showing us that. But please don't let that simple truth dull your sparkle. You were created to thrive in the face of inequity. That is the only answer to unfairness.

Thrive—just thrive.

8
APURL

YOU WILL BE TRANSFORMED

Transformation can be painful, but it is always worthwhile.

Life has a funny way of hitting hard. And when it does, just do the best you can. That is enough. Trust that no matter how tough this experience is for you, you will come out of it transformed.

Transformation changes caterpillars into butterflies, and it changes people into extraordinary human beings.

9
APRIL

JUDGMENT

Condemnation doesn't teach others a lesson. Instead, it hardens the heart and creates separation in the exact place that connection is needed.

When your first reaction is to disapprove of someone's choice, make an effort to be more kind instead. Withhold judgment. One day, it could be you making a choice someone else doesn't approve of.

10
APRIL

BE WILLING TO BE SURPRISED

"We must be willing to get rid of the life we've planned, so as to have the life that is waiting for us."

—JOSEPH CAMPBELL

If you were able to control each detail, you might feel safer. But the magic is often in the unknown; the beauty is in the surprises, and the grace is in the unexpected moments. Let go. Surrender. Ease up. Sit back and simply allow the magic to happen, and it will.

11
APRIL

~~~

SELF-COMPASSION FIRST

Compassion is the most generous gift you can give yourself. Show yourself the same mercy, sympathy, and kindness that you bestow upon others. It's difficult to show compassion toward others if you don't show it to yourself first.

Start with you, and then allow it to spread outward.

It will, I promise.

12
APRIL

~~~

YOU MATTER

You are heard.

You are seen.

Your life, your stories, and your experiences matter—perhaps more than you know.

Spread them far and wide.

13

APParts. APRIL

BUT IS IT TRUE?

Questioning your own reality can shift your perspective.

When you find yourself listening to the stories in your head, speaking negatively, or making judgments about others, ask yourself this simple question, without judgment: "Is it true?"

Is it possible that it is only your interpretation, rather than fact? Is there an opportunity to assume positive intention or have a more compassionate dialogue instead?

We are often assuming scenarios and judging others and ourselves, but having the ability to question ourselves gives us the opportunity to become more self-aware and openhearted.

14
APRIL

YOUR FEELINGS ARE ALWAYS RIGHT

When it comes to how you feel, you are always right. Do not question whether what you feel is acceptable or unacceptable. Whatever your feelings are, you are entitled to have them. Your feelings can be a window to your highest self—listen to them and honor them.

15
APRIL

YOU CAN FORGIVE WITHOUT ACCEPTING

You forgive in service of yourself, so that you will not be held hostage to negativity. Forgiveness is not acceptance; it's merely releasing something that doesn't serve you. Forgiveness doesn't mean that you consent to what occurred, only that you've consciously decided to let go in an effort to move forward with a sense of peace.

16
APRIL

YOU BELONG

You belong here. You may not always feel that way. Perhaps no one told you.

Right here—this is where your journey led you. You certainly belong here. Ground yourself in that knowledge, and take up more space than you think you deserve.

17
APRIL

BREAKDOWNS AND BEAUTY

There will be a time when the only way out is up: When all you can do to carry on is fall to your knees and cry the ugly cry, to break your heart wide open for whatever is to come next.

There will also be a time when the world will be so beautiful that the only way to take it all in is to fling your arms wide open, lift your face toward the sun, and allow all the beauty that exists to be one with your soul.

Both moments will come. Trust that you will be better for each of them.

18
APÍL

~~~

YOU ARE RARE

Show the world who you are. Be unconventional. Stand up for your individuality. Shine so brightly that you drown out the darkness.

    By doing so, you give others the permission to do the same. And you give the world the brilliant light it so desperately needs.

19
APRIL

~~~

COMPASSION WILL SHIFT YOU

Be more kind than you think is necessary. Offer your seat to a stranger. Smile. Say a loving word. Believe in others. Think generous thoughts. Your compassion will change the course of someone's life, and in the midst of that, it will change yours, too.

20
APALL

DO WHAT YOU LOVE IN THE ONE LIFE YOU'VE GOT

As cliché as this may sound, you can do what you love. Doing what you love is a choice and a commitment to yourself, with no excuses permitted.

Spend time losing yourself in what you enjoy. If you want to paint, paint. If you want to write, write. If you enjoy losing yourself in a novel, then read the book. If you want to walk barefoot in the grass, do that. Schedule it in if you must; set aside a few minutes daily or one day a week—whenever you can.

Just don't allow a lifetime to pass before you commit to doing the things you truly enjoy.

All the small moments add up and become the life you live. So, don't trudge through the moments, but turn them into the steps in the magnificent dance that is your life.

21

APRIL

~

YOU ARE POWERFUL

You are more capable than you know, more brilliant than you comprehend, and more powerful than you can even begin to understand.

22

APRIL

~

SELF-RESPECT

You show people how to treat you, and how you regard yourself is the example that you set for others to follow. Treat yourself with dignity, love, and forgiveness, and those around you will treat you with the same.

What you think of yourself matters greatly because it becomes the foundation for every decision you make. When you learn to love who you are, you free yourself from the binding expectations of others. Granting yourself that freedom is a powerful form of self-respect.

23
APRIL

YOU CAN'T POUR FROM AN EMPTY GLASS

When you feel like you are running on empty, you are. Trust that, and take a step back. Rest. Heal. Collect yourself. Then reconnect.

Only after you have refilled yourself will you be ready to dive back in and take over the world.

24
APRIL

THE WORLD IS WONDROUS

This big ol' crazy world is a wondrous place. Live as if you've got minutes left to admire it all. Expect beauty. Savor it—the light, colors, humor, and the full spectrum of the human experience. This is what it means to live, to allow yourself to truly be in the world.

Soak it in. There is no more extraordinary experience than exploring the world's wonder and truly living life in full color.

25
APRIL

LIFE IS BOTH

Sometimes you will lose. Often, you will win. Either way, you must accept what is.

    Honor all of it:
    The good and the not so good.
    The beautiful and the brutal.
    The peace and the unrest.
    The black and the white—and also the gray.
    The happiness and the anger.
    The delight and the sadness.

You are better for all of it—both this and that, as it is. No matter what life hands you, there are always profound lessons to be learned and opportunities awaiting. Don't ever forget that.

26
APRIL

WHEN THE ANSWERS DON'T COME

Regardless of how hard you try, there will be times when the answers you seek aren't ready to be discovered. When that happens—and it will—you are being called to allow your heart, intuition, and brain to catch up to one another. You must trust that the right answers will present themselves when you need them to. Have faith. Know that you will figure out the next step. But first, you must patiently sit with the questions.

27
APRIL

LOOK FORWARD

Looking back won't move you forward. Let the past go. Move on with the grace and wisdom that you've learned from every yesterday. Forgive yourself everything. You can't change what didn't happen or shift what did.

Instead, live in this moment, and look for all the beautiful possibility that today is filled with.

28
APRIL

LIVE YOUR OWN VERSION OF SUCCESS

Lots of folks will have well-intentioned opinions of what success looks like, but the only true version of success is the one you choose for yourself.

If your definition of success is money and material wealth, go for it. If it's living the lifestyle of a nomad or settling down in a small town and working a nine-to-five job, go for that. If it's following the path less traveled, do that. If it's following the path often trekked, then follow that path.

The choice is yours. There is no wrong version of success; there is only what success is to you. And don't forget that you can always change your vision of success, whether you're 20, 40, or 70 years old. The important thing is to always live your own version of a successful life.

29
APRIL

HAPPINESS TRAVELS

Happiness happens along the route; it's not a stop you get off at.

30
APRIL

AN EXERCISE IN STORIES: A STORY IS SIMPLY THAT

"A story, no matter how factually true, is still just a story."

—MARIANNE WILLIAMSON,
THE LAW OF DIVINE COMPENSATION

You decide the story you want to tell and the story you want to live. Oftentimes, they are not the same.

I grew up with a whole lot of love but very little money. I vividly remember making the decision as a 13-year-old that I wouldn't be a poor adult, I'd get an education, and I'd see the world. I've done all of those things.

Where I came from made me the woman I am, and though I will never forget that, I consciously choose to focus on the story of now. It's allowed me to keep moving forward rather than getting held back by what no longer exists.

What story are you choosing to tell? What story are you choosing to live in?

Think about that, and decide if that story is truly serving you today. Remember, no matter how true it is, it's still just another damn story.

MAY

1
MAY

LAUGHTER AND PLAY

Never let go of the child within. Be playful. Laugh often. Do things that don't make much sense to anyone else. Pick up rocks and seashells for no other reason than curiosity. Pull on your rubber boots and dance in the rain. Love easily. Hold hands with others. And don't ever take yourself so seriously that you forget how to be lighthearted in this big ol' crazy world.

2
MAY

JOY

Joy is a divine response to a life well lived, a lighting up from the inside out. It exists in spite of the burdens you carry and the troubles that arise in your life.

Your greatest responsibility may be giving yourself the permission to feel joy alongside grief. The depth of your joy can rise above sorrow. But first you must decide that it can.

3
MAY

~~~

CONTINUE

You owe it to yourself to be the highest expression of who you are—and to offer that self to every experience life brings you. You have a responsibility to live well, and when you get off track, to gently direct yourself back. Again, and again. Continue on your path with trust in yourself—that you will know the answers, that the answers will be revealed, that you will be okay, that you will thrive. Today, your only job is to continue.

4
MAY

~~~

COURAGEOUSLY STAND

Stand up for yourself and your beliefs. If you don't, neither will anyone else.

5
MAY

~~~

BACK HOME

You went left instead of right, your world shifted, and you lost touch with yourself. That's okay. You can always find your way back to the path of your heart by first accepting that you've gone astray. Patiently, graciously, and with all the love you gather, gently realign your actions with your heart to find your way back home.

6
MAY

YOU DON'T HAVE TO CARRY IT

A woman held up a glass of water and asked several of her colleagues what the weight was.

Someone ventured a guess: "20 ounces." Similar replies followed.

"Well," the woman said, "I can't know for certain unless I weigh it."

Then she asked, "What would happen if I held this glass for an hour?"

A colleague replied, "Your fingers and your arm might start to hurt."

"Good point!" she declared. "So what might happen if I held this glass up for a week?"

"Ha!" shouted another colleague, "Your arm would be numb, and you'd lose feeling in your upper back."

"Ah!" said the woman. "But the weight would never change, now, would it?"

This truth about the glass of water is also true of our burdens. We can choose to pick them up and carry them, feeling the weight every step of the journey, or we can decide to set them down from time to time.

Either way, what is, won't change. The only thing we gain from carrying our burdens around with us continuously is a bad back and a load of heartache, too. Let go of unnecessary burdens that erode your spirit. Amplify what brings you joy and happiness instead.

YOU WILL DO WELL

The path isn't linear; it's often zigzagged and crooked. The journey will sometimes feel like an uphill battle and, at other times, a downhill slide, depending on the moment.

Life may turn out differently than you expected, but it turns out exactly as it should. You will thrive; you will do well.

8
MAY
〜〜

DREAMS BECOME YOU

Your dreams are who you become. Visualize yourself living the life that you hope for, and hold that vision close. Remind yourself of it daily. Don't ever give up on it. You can achieve what you hope for only to the extent to which you can envision it.

9
MAY

EMBRACE THE ECCENTRICITIES

Embrace the quirks, the incongruities, and the inner wild that makes you, you.

Embody your truth: own it. Your weirdness is filled with wonder. Love all of who you are. In doing so, you offer yourself the one thing that no one else can give you: the beauty of true acceptance.

10
MAY

RISE UP

You are seen, and you are worthy. No matter where you come from or where you go, always stand tall with your shoulders back and your head held high. You deserve to be here.

Breathe deeply.
Root down.
Rise up.
Know that you belong wherever you choose to be.

11
MAY

~

AN EXERCISE IN BEING YOU

What would happen if you knocked down the proverbial fence that existed to keep you in line? What if you did what you enjoyed? What if you loved who you loved? What would it look like to live on the other side of the fence? Would you be a different person? How?

    Sit quietly and explore these questions from time to time. Give yourself the space to listen for what comes up, and then, based on that, do whatever you feel compelled to.

12
MAY

~

CREATE CHANGE WITH ACTION

Change begins with your thoughts and magnifies when you take action.

13
MAY

YOU ARE EXTRAORDINARY

You are extraordinary; accept this—in spite of what makes you different and because of what makes you different.

Do not adapt to become who others want you to be.

You will evolve, stretch, and grow, but still, as you are, you are extraordinary. In spite of all else, you are exactly who you are supposed to be: extraordinarily, genuinely you.

14
MAY

DON'T FEAR

Do not be afraid of your fears; they are simply there to show you what matters most to you.

15
MAY

BE COURAGEOUS ENOUGH TO BE YOURSELF

If you are courageous enough to be yourself in a world filled with the expectations of others, you will live a life with more joy, pleasure, and contentment (and a hell of a lot less regret).

16
MAY

IF NOT NOW, WHEN?

One day, you will wake up and decide that *now is the time*. The question is, what will it finally be the time for?

Write down this question to remind yourself what you've been waiting to do, see, or become in this lifetime. Acknowledge that now is the time, and then make that sh*t happen.

17
MAY

~~~

EMPOWERING OTHERS

Empower others to shine more brightly. Be kind, especially when it's most difficult. Believe in humanity. Show compassion and demonstrate empathy. Forgive others.

Doing these things won't always be easy, but in practicing these acts of humility, you awaken the possibility for others to do the same.

18
MAY

~~~

LEAVE TIME FOR CONTEMPLATION

Quiet contemplation allows you to connect with yourself, to remember who you are when the day is done, to ground down and breathe deeply.

Save 10 minutes each day to do nothing except spend time in your own company and contemplate your day.

19
MAY

INCOMPLETE SELF-COMPASSION

"If your compassion does not include yourself, it is incomplete."

—JACK KORNFIELD, *BUDDHA'S LITTLE INSTRUCTION BOOK*

20
MAY

LISTEN TO THE WISDOM OF OTHERS

Spend time in the company of those who challenge you to become more resilient, kind, and loving. Listen to the wisdom of others to expand your own. Especially listen to the wisdom of those who are different than you; they often have the most to teach you.

21
MAY

ALIGNMENT

To be in alignment is to allow yourself to believe that whatever you want is actually possible. To have faith in what you may not yet be able to visualize. To speak as if whatever you hope for already exists. To live in a way that invites your dreams to thrive. If you want love, be love; invite it in by offering it to others. If you seek joy, be joy; act in a way that is joyful, and allow others to experience it alongside you. Be what you hope for; allow whatever is on the inside to be how you live on the outside. This is true alignment.

22
MAY

BE CURIOUS

Curiosity will take you on adventures far and wide. Be open to it.

23
MAY

WAITING FOR APPROVAL

Are you still waiting for someone to tell you that you're doing it right (whatever "it" is)?

Okay, then here you go: You. Are. Doing. It. Right.

You are already doing it right. Keep doing it.

24
MAY

A MONTHLY POSITIVITY RITUAL

Write a list of five things that you enjoy doing—anything from visiting places you love to reading books that give you pleasure. Share the list with someone for accountability, and invite them to write their own list. Then, over the next 30 days, schedule time to do each of the items on your list. At the end of the month, share your experience with someone and then write the next month's list.

Repeat monthly.

Enjoy living a life filled with intentional moments.

25
MAY

IMAGINE THAT THIS MOMENT IS ALL YOU HAVE

What would you do differently if now is all you had? What words would you say to someone that you love? What actions might you take? What new things might you try if now was the only chance you had?

Now say, do, and act on whatever you answered above.

26
MAY

A MANTRA FOR ACCEPTING WHERE YOU ARE

"I am exactly where I am supposed to be."

27
MAY

CREATE A "LOVE + GOOD STUFF" FOLDER

When times are darkest, we easily forget all the kind things that people say about us. We forget who we are, and we sink into a place we don't want to be. This is exactly when a "Love + Good Stuff" folder comes in handy.

Create a folder. This can be a digital folder, paper folder, or box. Put into it cards, printed emails, kind notes and positive written words that anyone ever says about you. With your favorite marker or pen, label this folder "Love + Good Stuff" (or "Love + Good Sh*t").

Place your folder somewhere easily accessible. Add to it and review it as often as possible.

28

MAY

THE TRUTH ABOUT LOVE

"While infused with love you see fewer distinctions between you and others. Indeed, your ability to see others—really see them, wholeheartedly—springs open."

—BARBARA FREDRICKSON, PHD, *LOVE 2.0*

107

29
MAY

WHEN WALKING AWAY IS THE ANSWER

Sometimes leaving is the only option, because it is the only way to choose yourself. And when you choose yourself, you are consciously choosing to thrive in spite of the hurdles you will face by leaving.

When leaving is the only option, courage is your companion. Stand tall, accept your circumstances, and walk proudly toward your future. By choosing yourself, you will always triumph. Believe this in your heart.

30
MAY

A NOTE TO YOURSELF

Dear Self,

You deserve to be surrounded by people who lift you up and see your true beauty. You deserve genuine love, pure acceptance, and eternal patience. Please do not accept less than that.

I need you.

Love, Me

31

MAY

AN EXERCISE IN HAPPINESS

Ask yourself, "What does happiness mean to me? How could I add more happiness into my daily life? How could I treat myself better?"

Answer these questions. Then, ask yourself what you could change each day to add more happiness to your life.

Small changes can become powerful shifts.

Give it a try, and see how your happiness changes over the long term with some small, daily changes. If you find writing helpful to track these changes, start a happiness journal to record your answers and daily activities.

JUNE

1

JUNE

〜

YOU'VE NEVER GONE TOO FAR TO TURN BACK

Even if you've traveled miles in one direction, you can always turn around.

2

JUNE

〜

A MANTRA FOR GUILT

"I will not feel guilty for choosing myself first. Guilt is not welcomed here."

THE OLD FARMER

There was once an old farmer who had worked his crops for many years. One day, his horse ran away. Upon hearing the news, his neighbors came to visit.

"Such bad luck," they said sympathetically.

"Maybe," the farmer replied.

The next morning, the horse returned, bringing with it three other wild horses.

"How wonderful!" the neighbors exclaimed.

"Maybe," replied the old man.

The following day, his son tried to ride one of the untamed horses, was thrown, and broke his leg. The neighbors again came to offer their sympathy on his misfortune.

"Maybe," answered the farmer.

The day after, military officials came to the village to draft young men into the army. Seeing that the son's leg was broken, they passed him by. The neighbors congratulated the farmer on how well things had turned out.

"Maybe," said the farmer.

This Taoist story teaches us that fortune and misfortune are always a matter of perspective. Do you automatically see your circumstances as fortunate or unfortunate? Or are you, like the farmer, willing to wait and see?

4
JUNE

HOW TO GET STARTED

Doing anything of significance takes time, but you do have to start somewhere. Less talking, more doing. Take one small step and then another. If getting started means setting a simple intention, begin there. From intention comes action.

Whatever the first step is, don't wait. Get started.

5
JUNE

WHO DECIDES WHAT YOU DESERVE?

What do you deserve? How does it make you feel to say out loud what you deserve? If you didn't care what anyone else thought, then what might you deserve?

Are there consistencies or inconsistencies in your answers to the three previous questions? If so, notice them. Then, choose to acknowledge that what you deserve is your decision, and regardless of what you decide you deserve, you are worthy of it.

JUNE

AN EXERCISE FOR SHAME

Shame is a powerful emotion that you can use to your advantage. What are you ashamed of? Could you turn that shame into a powerful statement of acceptance instead?

For example, what if, instead of saying, "I am ashamed of growing up poor," you said, "Growing up in poverty is what has motivated me to work hard and have a deep appreciation for all that I own."

Using our shame this way allows us to thrive and move forward boldly. Give it a try.

JUNE

FOCUS ON THE ONES WHO LOVE YOU

Some people may not love you. Focus your energy on the ones who do. You'll be a whole lot happier because of it.

8

JUNE

~~~

MANIFEST

··

man·i·fest \ **ma-nə-fest** \ **adjective**

1. Readily perceived by the senses and especially by the sense of sight. **2.** Easily understood or recognized by the mind.

··

What you think becomes your words, and what you speak becomes your truth. Use your thoughts and words to manifest wisely.

9

JUNE

~~~

REGRET IS A WASTED EMOTION

Regret won't right any wrongdoing. As best you can, let go. Choose forgiveness and forge ahead, onward and upward.

LOVE IS FRIENDSHIP THAT HAS CAUGHT FIRE

"Love is friendship that has caught fire. It takes root and grows, one day at a time. Love is quiet understanding and mature acceptance of imperfection … [L]ove never steers you in the wrong direction. Love is elevating. It lifts you up. It makes you look up. It makes you better than you were before."

—ANN LANDERS, *CHICAGO TRIBUNE*, APRIL 18, 1998

11

JUNE

SMILE BEFORE YOU FEEL HAPPY

Smiling actually makes you happier—seriously.

Our brains are hardwired to understand that we smile when we encounter something positive. The brain releases endorphins and lowers our stress levels. By smiling during situations that are less exciting, we trick our brains into believing that we are experiencing something more desirable. That, in turn, makes us feel happier.

Try smiling in situations that seem monotonous, boring, or even difficult.

12

JUNE

BE PRESENT

There are few things as precious as being present in this moment. So pay close attention to the subtleties of what surrounds you, and experience the majesty of living in the present moment. Move more slowly. Witness the subtle smile. Breathe in the scent of the flowers. Hear the laughter.

13
JUNE

PERMISSION IS YOURS TO GRANT

Stop waiting for permission to be yourself. Not a single person has the right to grant you that permission except for you.

14
JUNE

POSITIVITY

Smile. Say a kind word. Believe in the goodness of strangers. Think positively. Trust that better times are ahead. Do something nice for yourself. Empower others to live more boldly. Small shifts in positivity make for much more sustainable long-term happiness.

15
JUNE

~~~

TOMORROW IT MAY NOT MATTER

What seems important today, in this moment, may not matter at all tomorrow.

What are some experiences that caused you a lot of worry but eventually turned out to be much less significant than you'd expected? Write them down on a piece of paper titled "Things That Didn't Really Matter All That Much."

When a new situation feels bigger than you, return to this list for a dose of much-needed perspective.

16
JUNE

~~~

REPLACE FEAR

What if you replaced fear with curiosity, excitement, and optimism?

For example, you could change "I'm afraid to try this because I've never done it before" to "I'm so curious about this. I'm excited to give it a whirl."

See the difference in this simple mind-set shift? Try it out for yourself.

17
JUNE

LOOKING BACK AND MOVING FORWARD

Be careful not to stay stranded in the past. Do not look back unless it is to recognize how far you've moved forward. Use the wisdom you gathered from the past, and quietly advance in the direction of your wildest dreams.

18
JUNE

BELIEVE THAT YOU CAN

If he did it, why can't you? If she did it, why not you?
    If they did it, so could you.
    Believe that you can, and you will.

19
JUNE

A LETTER OF GRATITUDE

Gratitude is especially powerful when directed toward others.

Write a letter to someone who positively impacted you. Perhaps they said a kind word when you needed it most, or they showed you love when you couldn't yet love yourself. Write them a detailed note thanking them.

Notice how it feels to write this letter. How long afterward do you still feel gratitude?

If you feel compelled, give them the letter. However, know that you can still feel the impact of gratitude whether you choose to give them the letter or not.

Consider making this practice a monthly ritual.

20
JUNE

LOVE YOURSELF

Love yourself first so that you can teach others how you want to be loved.

21
JUNE

~~~

WHERE THE LIGHT IS

You can't see the stars without the darkness.

22
JUNE

~~~

A MANTRA FOR TAKING BACK CONTROL

"I am responsible for my life, my feelings, and the environment, both the good and the bad. I will surround myself in positivity."

When you feel at a loss for all that is happening around you, assert responsibility for your life by using this mantra.

23
JUNE

~

BEING THANKFUL

Gratitude allows you to temporarily step away from life's struggles.

As you wake up each day, name five things you are thankful for. Write them in a bedside journal. Consider sharing this list with others, both online and in person.

24
JUNE

~

KEEP GOING

Keep putting one foot in front of the other. You may fall, but you will also eventually find your way forward. Don't give up. Keep going. Keep moving. Take one step, then another, until you arrive.

25
JUNE

AN EXERCISE IN FORGIVENESS

Forgive yourself; whatever you did is done. Especially forgive yourself for all that you've taken responsibility for that you didn't actually do. You can't make anyone feel anything; you did the best you could. Forgive yourself and move forward.

26
JUNE

YOU HAVE THE RIGHT TO BE HERE

You belong. You are loved. You are needed. You belong here.

27

JUNE

AN EXERCISE IN APPRECIATION

Write a list of the people who matter most in your life. Take your time, and consider why they mean so much to you. Write these reasons down under their names.

Then, when you are able, pick up the phone. Tell them that they are important to you and why. Notice how you feel afterward.

28

JUNE

WHERE TRUE HAPPINESS LIES

True happiness begins the moment you decide to be yourself. The moment you accept all of who you are, despite your imperfections, you realize that happiness has been awaiting you all along.

29

JUNE

MAKE MISTAKES

You are human; you will make mistakes. Hopefully, you'll make a whole lot of them, because that means you are trying, and trying means you are fully alive. It also makes life a hell of a lot more interesting.

30

JUNE

THE MIRROR BECOMES YOU

Value your life. Believe in what is possible. Love yourself more. Trust your heart. The one person that will impact your life most is in the reflection of your mirror.

JULY

1
JULY

~

LIVE YOUR OWN TRUTH

Live your own wild truth in whatever way serves you. Be a rebel. With every breath in your body, remind yourself that you can do all the things you've ever been told that you couldn't. You're an adult, and you get to decide what to do and how to do it.

Go, do, and rise.

2
JULY

~

TOLERANCE

Courageously take the time to notice your own self-righteousness. It limits how loving and accepting you can become.

Listen to the stories of others. Be more accepting of people who think differently than you do. That doesn't mean that you have to change your beliefs, but it does mean that you have to accept the beliefs of others without judgment or defensiveness. Everyone deserves the right to be who they truly are—including you.

3
JULY

~~~

AN EXERCISE IN SHOULD

Write a list of all the things you think you should do. Don't overthink it.

Then, ask yourself who said you should do each of these things.

We often reprimand ourselves for not doing things that we never actually consciously chose to do at all. These "shoulds" can be rooted in guilt or obligation, and oftentimes, they are the result of beliefs that others have placed upon us.

Are decisions you make today out of perceived obligation still serving the life you currently lead or want to lead?

Returning to your list of shoulds, cross off anything that no longer serves the life you lead today. Then, take a deep breath and enjoy the freedom of deciding for yourself what you want and need to do.

4
JULY

~~~

A MANTRA FOR SELF LOVE AND ACCEPTANCE

"I love myself unconditionally, and the world around me is as it should be."

5
JULY

~~~

SPEAK IT INTO EXISTENCE

"Words are, in my not so humble opinion, our most inexhaustible source of magic."

—J.K. ROWLING

Speak your dreams out loud, as if they were already true. Believe in them and remind yourself of them daily.

When you do, the world around you will begin to co-create the vision of reality that you had the courage to speak aloud.

6
JULY

~~~

RESENTMENT WON'T SERVE YOU

Resentment has no good purpose. Unfortunately, the only one who feels the destructive effect of its power is the one who is resentful. As best you can, let it go.

7
JULY

YOU ARE TOO BIG FOR BOXES

Do not shrink to fit into boxes that are too small to contain all of your magnificence.

8
JULY

OPTIMISM IS NOT SELF-DECEPTION

"[Optimism] is not about providing a recipe for self-deception. The world can be a horrible, cruel place, and at the same time it can be wonderful and abundant. These are both truths. There is not a halfway point; there is only choosing which truth to put in your personal foreground."

—SONJA LYUBOMIRSKY,
(QUOTING LEE ROSS), *THE HOW OF HAPPINESS*

9
JULY

BRAVERY IS A MUSCLE YOU CAN BUILD

Fear is unnerving and rattles you into complacency. Do not allow it to.
Keep moving forward. One foot and then the next until you move beyond
that scary place. The more you challenge fear, the bolder you become.

10
JULY

YOU ARE ENOUGH

You are more enough than you can even conceive in this moment. You
are brilliant. Every day, you are brighter and more resilient than you were
yesterday. Remind yourself often that exactly as you are, you are enough.

11
JULY

~~

AN EXERCISE TO RECALL YOUR BEST SELF

We spend much of our time thinking about our imperfections. If we spent that same time thinking about what is right about ourselves, our ideas, visions, and plans might then have the space they need to crystallize.

Set a timer, and spend 20 minutes writing about your best self. List all of your positive traits. Keep writing until the timer goes off.

Then, spend 10 minutes writing about the traits you'd like to embody (such as patience), and speak them out loud in first person "I am" statements: "I am patient."

12
JULY

~~

YOU ARE STRONGER THAN YOUR SHAME

Whatever you are most ashamed of can also be the source of great resilience, and ultimately, strength. You are stronger than your shame. Always remember this.

13
JULY

ALLOW YOURSELF TO HOPE AND DREAM

No matter how broken the world may seem, allow yourself to continue to dream of a better way. You are strong, and your spirit will rise to every mountaintop as long as you allow it to. Keep believing in what is possible, even if you can't quite visualize it yet. Without your hope and dreams, what else is there to look forward to?

The energy and intentions behind your hopes and dreams carry magic. Allow it to occur and be open to our dreams coming true.

14
JULY

BOUNDARIES ARE HEALTHY

Healthy boundaries teach people how to treat you. Respect what you need and trust your intuition. Don't be afraid to share your boundaries with others instead of closing yourself off. By nurturing healthy relationships they become more functional, loving and supportive for each person.

15
JULY

CHOOSE BEAUTY

Focus on the beauty in life, and that is what you will most often experience. The opposite is also true.

16
JULY

THE WORLD NEEDS YOUR UNIQUENESS

Be exactly who you are. The things that make you different are also what make you incredible. The world does not need more people to think and act like everyone else. Ideas, acceptance, and the depth of true inner beauty are all born from uniqueness. Hone the confidence that you need to stand out from others, and every day you will become more of who you genuinely are.

17
JULY

GRIEVE

Grieve in whichever way you feel compelled to. There isn't one right way to move through what saddens you. Give yourself the space to feel. Be sad. Be angry. Be heartbroken. Cry or don't. But also take deep breaths and remember the love that brought you to your knees, the smiles that broke your heart wide open, and the moments of laughter and joy. Finding the happiness among the grief can make each difficult moment a bit easier to bear. Show yourself more love than you've ever needed to before, and feel what you feel.

18
JULY

COURAGEOUSLY SPEAK YOUR TRUTH

There is someone else who needs exactly what only you can say. Share what you believe with courage. Say it out loud. When you speak your truth, you set an example for others to speak theirs as well.

19
JULY

LET GO NOW

Let go of that thing that you've held on to for far too long: that emotion that keeps you closed off, that job that makes you feel lost inside, or that person who doesn't serve your highest self. Whatever it is that you find yourself begrudgingly holding on to, let it go. Even if letting go means just taking the first step in the direction of change. Go toward it. Letting go will look different for each of us, and letting go is a process.

   Not sure what it is you need to let go of? Take a long, deep breath, look directly into a mirror, and ask yourself. Speaking to our own image has a way of bringing to awareness the things that may be hidden in your unconscious.

20
JULY

HOW TO LIVE A WONDERFUL LIFE

Choose joy. Practice love. Accept others. Be kind. Show respect. Love yourself. Repeat.

21
JULY

~~

AN EXERCISE IN LETTING GO OF FEAR

Fear prevents you from showing up in your greatest capacity. Instead of letting fear dictate your circumstance, use it to shift you forward into uncharted territory.

Without judgment, list everything that you are afraid of, from the (seemingly) unimportant to your greatest fears.

Choose five fears, and decide on two action steps that you can take to move toward letting each fear go. Repeat as often as necessary.

22
JULY

YOU ARE NOT ALONE

Even during your darkest times, know that you are not alone. You've never been alone. You are loved, and you've always been loved. You are needed. You have purpose. You matter.

23
JULY

A MANTRA FOR DOING WHAT FEELS IMPOSSIBLE

There will be times when it feels impossible to do the thing you believe in— moments when you simply cannot take a step forward.

First, show yourself patience. And when you are ready, remind yourself that the only person who can talk you into believing in your power is you.

Say the following mantra repeatedly throughout your day. Use it as often as possible, and write it down on sticky notes throughout your home as a daily reminder:

"I am incredibly powerful. I can do this. I will do this."

24

JULY

~

KNOW IT

If you think you can, you might. If you know you can, you will.

25

JULY

~

CONFIDENCE AND INSECURITIES

The person you are looking at as a model of perfection may also be looking toward someone else for that very same reason. Everyone has insecurities, and no one is perfect. But that doesn't mean you shouldn't strive to accept who you are, without condition.

Insecurities make you human, but acceptance transforms insecurity into confidence.

26
JULY

STAY OPEN TO WONDER

The world is filled with awe and beauty.

Marvel at the ordinary, and witness the wonder that lies beneath the surface. Be open to fresh perspectives and new ideas, and be curious. Widen your own horizon by learning from others.

Expand, discover, and thrive with your heart wide open to wonder.

27
JULY

LOVE AGAIN

Don't ever give up on love. It may not always be perfect, and you may experience it many times or few. But don't ever let that stop you from being willing to love again.

28
JULY

~~

THE DETERMINING FACTOR

"Life shrinks or expands in proportion to one's courage."

—ANAÏS NIN

29
JULY

~~

DON'T FORGET YOUR DREAMS

Allow your dreams to blossom, and get out of your own way.
Repeat to yourself, "Today I grant myself permission to dream."

30

JULY

WORRYING DOESN'T CHANGE ANYTHING

It is human nature to worry about what you care deeply for, but worrying alone does not change anything. All you get in return is sleepless nights, scattered thoughts, and a whole lot of heartbreak.

Think about how you can better channel your concerns. What actions can you take to support what you are worried about? Who can help you carry the weight of whatever is keeping you awake at night?

You cannot change what you have no control over, but you'll feel a lot more powerful if you take direct action around what you are able to shift. Remember: Action creates transformation, but worrying simply creates more anguish.

31

JULY

THE WORLD OVERFLOWS WITH KINDNESS

The world is filled with kindness. Seek it out, and you will repeatedly find it.

AUGUST

WHEN TO ACCEPT AND WHEN TO LET GO

Accept what you can impact, and let go of what you cannot change.

AUGUST

NURTURE RELATIONSHIPS OF INTEGRITY

You do not need to have the same interests or personalities as those you surround yourself with. What matters is that you connect from your heart and that you value the integrity of your connection equally. Sustain relationships that take you outside of your comfort zone; they will support your growth. Foster these friendships and they will bring you more joy, love, and connection than you ever knew possible. Relationships built of integrity will carry you through both the best and the worst of times. Always create space for them.

3
AUGUST

ALWAYS CHOOSE HAPPINESS

Every single day and every single moment, you are given the opportunity to choose happiness over despair. Choose happiness.

4
AUGUST

A BEAUTIFUL LIFE ISN'T A PERFECT ONE

The most beautiful life is the one you choose for yourself. Decide how you want to spend your time, and then do that. Even when your life doesn't go according to plan, know that you've chosen a life that suits you. And remember that a beautiful life isn't necessarily a perfect one.

STAY OPEN TO THE MAGIC OF LIFE

Life is not boring, unless you allow it to be. There is magic everywhere—from the sidewalk rainbow after a rainstorm to the casual run-in with a long-lost friend to a smile received from a perfect stranger. Notice how often you hear from someone you've been thinking about or how you find just the right words to say in the moment you need them most. This is magic that can easily be missed. Practice noticing it. Keep your heart and your eyes open wide enough to appreciate the synchronicities and magic around you.

AUGUST

YOU ARE NOT BROKEN

You do not need to be fixed, nor do you need to become someone else's version of perfection. You are a human being experiencing the highest of highs and the lowest of lows. Accept that you are not damaged. You will sometimes feel broken and sometimes feel more together than you ever dreamed possible. But either way, you are an extraordinarily complete person—strong, vulnerable, and alive. You, my dear, are not broken; you are exceptionally human.

7
AUGUST

EXTRAORDINARILY SIMPLE

"The simple things are also the most extraordinary things, and only the wise can see them."

—PAULO COELHO

8
AUGUST

AN EXERCISE IN SELF-KINDNESS

Treat yourself. Eat well. Relax. Move more slowly. Be kind. Spend 10 minutes writing a few kind words about yourself on small pieces of paper. Place these notes in unexpected places, like in your wallet, on your bathroom cabinet, and in your favorite coffee mug. Finding them later will offer reminders of how extraordinary you truly are.

MIRROR WHAT YOU HOPE FOR

Embody the changes you wish to see around you.

AN EXERCISE IN PERSPECTIVE

Write a letter to your future self: Tell yourself who you are today, what your greatest fears are, and what you believe in. What are your goals? What do you hope to get even better at? Give yourself advice, and share life lessons.

Seal up the letter, and store it in a safe place. Set a reminder on your calendar to mail the letter to yourself one to three years from today. (Yes, mail it.)

Years from now, you will open the letter and discover the perspective that can only come with time.

11
AUGUST

HEALING NEEDS TRUST

Only time heals. And even when time passes, we are not always healed in the way we hoped to be. However, we will be healed in the way we need to be. Trust that you will be okay, even if being okay today looks different than it did before.

12
AUGUST

FEEL HOWEVER YOU FEEL

Feel what you feel. Do not attempt to be happy in every moment of sadness. Happiness is a powerful emotion, but it needs space in order to thrive. Sadness also needs space to be felt before it can move along and make way for other emotions.

Allow yourself to feel all emotions with compassion. Know that these feelings, too, shall pass. And when you are ready, trust that you will gracefully move forward.

13
AUGUST

~~~

RELEASE WHAT YOU NO LONGER NEED

Surrender the parts of your past that no longer serve you. People, possessions, thoughts—be willing to release them if you don't need them anymore. Doing so creates the space you need to allow in true love, to create honest connection, and to live an extraordinarily fulfilled life.

14
AUGUST

~~~

RISE

Stand tall, rise up, and the world will meet you there.

15
AUGUST

PUT YOURSELF IN THE WAY OF BEAUTY

"There's always a sunrise and always a sunset and it's up to you to choose to be there for it. Put yourself in the way of beauty."

—CHERYL STRAYED (QUOTING HER MOTHER), *WILD*

16
AUGUST

CONTENTMENT IS A CHOICE

Contentment is like a big ol' hug at the end of a hard day; you inhale deeply, and everything else disappears around you. It's a satisfaction, joy, and ease that you experience when you decide that what you have is plenty. The one caveat is that you are the only person who decides whether contentment is possible or impossible.

17
AUGUST

YOU DECIDE

Life is exactly what you make of it. What are you making of your life? Are there changes you'd like to make? If so, what are they? And what steps can you take to move in that direction?

18
AUGUST

~

A MANTRA FOR SELF-WORTH

"I am powerful. I am divine. I am extraordinary, and I am worthy of all the good stuff this world has to offer."

19
AUGUST

~

SHAME

"Shame is the lie someone told you about yourself."

—ANAÏS NIN

20
AUGUST

~~~

YOUR DREAMS ARE READY

Every hard-earned lesson that you've ever experienced brought you to this exact place. You are meant to be here. You have everything that you need now and will need in the future. The only thing missing from your dreams is you. Now is the time to leap and then soar into the life you've always hoped for.

21
AUGUST

~~~

THIS IS SELF-CONFIDENCE

You'll be okay, even if they don't like you. You like you. And that is the greatest gift that you'll ever bestow upon yourself.

22
AUGUST

~

THE ONLY PLACE TO GO IS UP

Sometimes the bottom is exactly where you have to reach before you can rise higher than you ever have before.

23
AUGUST

~

AN EXERCISE IN UNDERSTANDING YOURSELF

What words do you need to hear right now? Write them down.

What do you love about who you are? Write it down.

What lessons have you learned from the challenges you've overcome?

Keep writing. You have the power to give yourself what you need in any moment. Remind yourself of your own resilience, greatness, and power. Who better to teach you how extraordinary you are than you?

24
AUGUST

ADVERSITY IS NECESSARY, TOO

Though it may not be comfortable, adversity teaches you resilience and courage. It teaches you to hold on tightly to what matters most and to surrender what doesn't. It is the anchor to humanity that prevents you from flying too far, too fast, and scorching yourself on the sun. For all the beauty in life—and life is indeed beautiful—you still need the balance of adversity to grow stronger, so you can live a more meaningful life.

25
AUGUST

NEW BEGINNINGS

Every new beginning comes from the end of something else. This is the natural ebb and flow of life, and it asks us to accept that happiness often lies on the other side of sadness. Know that there is always an opportunity to begin again as soon as you allow yourself to.

26
AUGUST

YOU ARE WHO YOU SAY YOU ARE

No one gets to decide how empowered you are except for you. Take center stage, and accept the spotlight. Lead by example. Do what makes you proud. Shine brightly, and courageously show us how it's done. Decide to show up in the world as the empowered, powerful being that you are.

27
AUGUST

THE POWER OF SELF-COMPASSION

"Having compassion starts and ends with having compassion for all those unwanted parts of ourselves, all those imperfections that we don't even want to look at. Compassion isn't some kind of self-improvement project or ideal that we're trying to live up to."

—PEMA CHÖDRÖN, *WHEN THINGS FALL APART*

28
AUGUST

~

AN EXERCISE IN MOVEMENT AND HAPPINESS

List five songs that make you wildly happy. Do not judge what the songs are; simply write them down. Set aside 10 minutes a week and dance to them. Don't worry about who might watch you. Move your hips and smile.

Give it a try, and notice how it makes you feel.

It's very difficult to dance and be miserable at the same time, I promise.

29
AUGUST

~

TRYING IS NOT PERFECTION

Try new things and be willing to fail. Don't worry about the end result; just put in the effort. Let go of expectation: whatever happens is happening as it should. Challenge your own beliefs. Do the thing that feels difficult. The only way you'll arrive at the magic is if you willingly travel a few challenging roads to get there.

30
AUGUST

REGRET DOESN'T SERVE YOU

Regret won't serve you as life passes you by. While you can, kiss more and love with all your heart, even if it may get broken. Forgive even when it hurts. Surrender and move on. Worry less. Travel more. Spend more time with the ones you adore and less time with the ones you don't. Don't work too hard. Make time for yourself. Above all else, live a life you're proud of, and release all regrets.

31
AUGUST

FALL APART

Sometimes we have to fall apart in order to rebuild with a stronger foundation. It's never too late to be who you want to be and live a life that you are proud of, even if that means beginning again.

And you can always begin again.

SEPTEMBER

1

SEPTEMBER

A MANTRA FOR ABUNDANCE

*"I have everything I need—
financially, emotionally, and physically.
I am overflowing with prosperity
and happiness."*

2

SEPTEMBER

PRACTICE POSITIVITY

Look for the good in every experience and, as best you can, find the lessons in each setback. Celebrate wins. Seek out the bright side. Surround yourself with positive people and environments. Being optimistic takes practice. Optimism may not work all the time, but the more you practice thinking positively, the more optimism becomes second nature.

AN EXERCISE IN CONFIDENCE

When you're trying to be humble, it's easy to forget how extraordinary you are.

Make a list of your best qualities. Feel free to be generous with your praise. Brag! You don't always have to be humble. Reminding yourself of your abilities and positive traits is an act of empowerment, not arrogance.

Then, turn your list into a series of affirmations by adding "I am" before each one: *I am incredibly generous. I am beautiful. I am a great parent. I am a loyal friend.*

Say your affirmations out loud to yourself. Take it one step further and record yourself speaking these affirmations. Whenever you need to, listen to the voice recording to remind yourself of your own brilliance.

YOU MAY NEVER BE READY

You may never be ready, but that isn't a good reason not to start.

WHEN THINGS DON'T GO AS PLANNED

For better or worse, life will not always go as planned. When you're experiencing a challenge, rather than assuming the worst possible scenario, ask yourself what you could learn from it. What in this challenge could make you stronger, more loving, or more empathetic? Sit with what comes up, and have a notebook nearby to record your thoughts.

You won't always find the answer you want to hear but you'll begin to recognize that things are not always as negative as they may seem initially.

AN EXERCISE IN ASSUMING POSITIVITY

"Life is simple. Everything happens for you, not to you."

—BYRON KATIE, *A THOUSAND NAMES FOR JOY*

What if you assumed that everything in your life is working for you rather than against you? Would that change your actions? How? Why?

Assuming positivity will allow you to trust outcomes, regardless of whether they are perceived to be good or bad.

7
SEPTEMBER

LET IT GO

Yesterday is done. The words were said, the actions were taken, and the feelings were felt. Forgive. Let yesterday go, and move boldly forward with the wisdom of lessons learned.

8
SEPTEMBER

A MANTRA FOR OPTIMISM

"Things will always work out. I may not know exactly how, but I know that somehow, eventually, things will work out for the best."

9

DARE TO BE YOURSELF

Stand up and show the world who you are. Your most genuine self is not the self that seeks to fit in; it is the part of you that is wild, unexpected, and extraordinary. Own that part of you. Show yourself the acceptance and respect that you deserve, and in so doing, you will be asking the same of others. It takes courage to be unapologetic about who you are. Be courageous and do it anyway.

It's powerful to be in the company of someone who accepts themselves fully, flaws and all. They stand taller with their head held high—majestic. They know who they are and they own that. Today is your turn to own it.

Who are you really? What about yourself do you withhold from others out of shame, judgment, or embarrassment? Write yourself a note detailing your answers. Can you take a stand for who you are by sharing some part of that with someone else?

Dare to be the most authentic version of yourself, and so, too, will others. Enjoy the freedom that comes from deep self-acceptance and self-love. You are worthy of it.

10
SEPTEMBER

YOU DESERVE IT

You deserve to smile. You deserve to laugh. You deserve love. You deserve to experience happiness. You deserve all the goodness that the world has to offer.

11
SEPTEMBER

EVERYTHING IS TEMPORARY

Autumn transitions into winter. The young get older. Caterpillars change into butterflies. This is life. Everything shifts, and each experience is temporary.

Enjoy what is, individual and fleeting as it may be. Avoid clinging. Surrender gracefully when change comes, because it will. And when it does, know that you, too, will shift, but you will always be okay.

12
SEPTEMBER

THE POWER OF SELF-TALK

The most important conversations you will ever have are the ones you have internally. What you say to yourself becomes your truth.

Praise yourself often and share your successes with others. Speak about yourself with patience, forgiveness, and love. Humility and pride are not at odds with each other; you can be humble and still be proud of your accomplishments.

What you say to yourself inwardly affects the way you experience life outwardly. Be kind with your words to yourself, because they are incredibly powerful.

13
SEPTEMBER

~

THE ANSWERS WILL COME

You are not stuck; you are temporarily at a loss for answers. To be stuck is to feel hopeless, rudderless. But you, my love, have hope, and you know that the answers will present themselves when the time is right. Be patient, and trust that the answers will come. They always do.

14
SEPTEMBER

~

START FRESH

Your past has passed. When you are called to release whatever you've held on to for far too long, let go. Surrender as best you can, and start anew. How exciting! You can begin again in whichever way you choose; revel in this idea. Then, prepare yourself for the energy of bright, brand-new beginnings.

15

SEPTEMBER

ANGER IS TOO HEAVY A BURDEN

Anger is a heavy burden that will wear you down and keep you from seeing better days ahead. Holding on to anger is too difficult, and carrying it will not make you happier. Create change where you can, and correct whichever wrongs you are able to. But then, release the anger and instead choose contentment, peace of mind, and hope for the future.

16

SEPTEMBER

GET COMFORTABLE WITH THE WORD NO

Saying no leaves room for the right yes to come along.

17

SEPTEMBER

YOU WILL BECOME WHOLE ONCE AGAIN

Difficult times will come, but they will also pass. You will fall apart sometimes, because you are human. When those times come, grieve, cry, and feel whatever you feel for as long as you need to. And whenever you're ready, remind yourself that you will become whole once again. Because you will.

18

SEPTEMBER

YOU ARE NOT INVISIBLE

You are heard, even if no one acknowledges what you said. You matter, even if you don't speak the loudest. You are seen by others, even if you don't realize it. You do matter, and you are not invisible.

YOU ARE NOT YOUR HARDSHIPS

Difficult times do not define you. They develop your strength, and they hone your resilience. Even in the worst of times, there is always a way forward, but first you must decide that you are more than your struggles. When you do, you will become wiser and more self-aware because of your experiences, not in spite of them. You will also learn that you are so much more than any of your difficulties.

MISTAKES MAKE YOU

*"You don't make mistakes.
Mistakes make you.
Mistakes make you smarter.
They make you stronger, and
they make you more self-reliant."*

—SHIRLEY MACLAINE, AS HARRIET LAULER, IN *THE LAST WORD*

Do not live in fear of what you have done wrong. Learn the lesson, grab the opportunities that arise because of your mistakes, and then gracefully move on. This is how you grow.

21
SEPTEMBER

~~~

PERMISSION GRANTED TO GIVE IN

There will be times when your best option is to simply give in—when peace of mind is more important than needing to be right, when softening inwardly and accepting things as they are is the only way. When surrendering feels like the best option, it probably is.

22
SEPTEMBER

~~~

FIND HOPE

Find hope in healing. Whether you are healing from a broken heart or a broken spirit, there is always hope.

WATCH CAREFULLY

*"Watch your thoughts, they become words;
watch your words, they become actions;
watch your actions, they become habits;
watch your habits, they become character;
watch your character, for it becomes your destiny."*

—FRANK OUTLAW, FOUNDER OF BI-LO SUPERMARKET CHAIN

AN EXERCISE IN BREATHING

Having the ability to breathe is what gives us life. And because breathing seems so natural for many of us, we forget the power our breath has.

Take deep breaths often. When you find yourself anxious, angry, or simply deflated, try this breathing technique to bring yourself back to a place of calm.

Inhale and exhale fully. Then, take a deep inhale and visualize a white ball of light moving up your spine. Hold the breath for two seconds, if it's comfortable. Then, as you exhale, visualize that same white light moving down your spine. Repeat for 10 rounds, allowing each breath to get a tiny bit longer on each round. Notice the difference you feel afterward.

Note: This exercise should not feel uncomfortable. If taking longer breaths makes it challenging for you to breathe, please do not lengthen your breath while using this technique. Instead, just breathe normally using the same visualization, and the breath will slow naturally on its own.

25
SEPTEMBER

PRIORITIZE

"If you don't prioritize your own life,
someone else will."

—GREG MCKEOWN, *ESSENTIALISM*

Prioritize what matters most. Decide how you want to spend your life—every moment. Kiss your children, love your friends, speak kindly to strangers, hold hands with your loved ones, and go for walks. These will be the things you remember when all you have left is today.

26

SEPTEMBER

SCRIBBLE ALL OVER THE PAGE

Don't take yourself so seriously that you forget what it feels like to belly laugh so hard that you cry. Leave the bed unmade and go play. Paint. Get messy. Go outside barefoot. Sketch outside of the lines in the brightest colored pencils that you can find. Hold hands quietly instead of rushing to wash the dishes after a meal. Accept open invitations from friends and stop by for a cup of tea or a shared bottle of wine. Watch movies that make you happy. Get lost in a good novel. Be a bit less serious, and enjoy what you have.

27

SEPTEMBER

YOU CAN'T CONTROL IT

Let go of the need to control every detail of your existence, because life will happen whether you control it or not. How much fun you have while you're in the midst of it all is entirely up to you.

28
SEPTEMBER

ASSUME GOODWILL

Most people are genuinely kindhearted and considerate. Always assume goodwill. When you allow your default to be positive intention, you will quickly notice that your perspective shifts to one of more positivity overall.

29
SEPTEMBER

ALLOW ROOM FOR PAUSE

We live in a world of constant activity that leaves us feeling overcharged. But there is so much power in stillness. What would happen if you slowed down? Would the world around you feel different?

Try it. Slow down. Breathe in. Look outward. See inward. Exhale. Repeat as often as needed.

30

SEPTEMBER

PROVING YOURSELF TO EVERYONE ELSE IS FUTILE

You are your greatest advocate, and the validation that you need most is your own. You are strong enough and good enough, exactly as you are in this moment, to do whatever you choose to do. Even if others are well intentioned with their advice, only you know what is best for you. So stay true to your choices and trust in your strength. Find happiness in whichever way suits you. The people you are trying your hardest to impress are likely not your people. The ones who deserve your respect and attention are the ones who see you as you are and love you anyway.

OCTOBER

1

OCTOBER

LIFE WILL GET BACK TO NORMAL

When difficult times arise, remind yourself that life will go back to normal, even if it's a new normal. Whatever you are experiencing will eventually pass. This truth doesn't diminish what is happening, but it allows you to find the light at the end of the tunnel by recognizing that time will keep moving forward. And in time, you will be okay once again.

2

OCTOBER

OWN YOUR WEIRDNESS

Committing to authentically being who you are will not always be easy. It takes courage and heart to be who you were born to be. But you'll have a lot more fun, and you'll find your true place of belonging if you do.

3
OCTOBER

PERCEIVE BEAUTY IN THE WORLD

Expect the world to be a beautiful place, and it will be. Find beauty in small details and the big ones, too.

4
OCTOBER

THE SUN ALWAYS PEEKS THROUGH

The rain will come and so will the rainbows. Trust that no matter the storm, you can weather it. And know that no matter how bad a situation may seem, the sun will always find its way through.

AN EXERCISE IN EMPOWERMENT

It is empowering to know our own strengths and to understand the impact that we have on those around us. But it can be difficult for us to see what is positive and valuable about ourselves. Those who love us are often able to recognize these traits much more clearly than we do.

Send a message to five of your closest friends or family members, and ask them to list five of your most positive traits. When you read their responses, what do you feel? Do you believe them? Why or why not? How does it feel to know that people think about you this way?

Do not judge their responses or yours; just pay close attention to how you feel.

LIVING THE GOOD LIFE

A good life is not something that just happens to you. You choose it as much as it chooses you.

You decide to live well every day with every single decision you make.

You love. You dream. You fail.

You fall. And eventually, you get up.

You try again. And maybe again.

You stand tall.

You shift.

You grow.

You create.

Because you made the conscious choice to live a good life, to live well—whatever that means to you.

7
OCTOBER

~

ALLOW YOUR PAST TO HEAL YOU

You've become who you are because of every experience you have ever endured—the trauma and the beauty. When you allow it to, your past creates empathy for the experiences of others and an overwhelming sense of possibility for yourself. Your past can heal you and prepare you for a more resilient future, but only if you give it permission to. You can consciously decide how heavy or light you will allow the weight of your past to be.

8
OCTOBER

~

HALF FULL

As you move through your day, keep in mind that experiencing your situation as negative or positive—as a glass half empty or half full—is entirely up to you. Which will you choose?

Look back on the past 48 hours. How could you have viewed your situation as half full or, in other words, more positively? How can that previous experience be a lesson for how you view the world today?

EXPERIENCE YOUR LIFE THROUGH THE LENS OF A TOURIST

Imagine everything around you as if it were the very first time you've ever seen it.

The excitement, laughter, joy, and love. The beauty in every detail. The nuance of the colors and the play of shadows and light. The breathtaking views of the city or the rural landscape, the cracks in the sidewalks, the trees and the individual blades of grass, the sunshine and rain.

Everything can be miraculous. Shifting to the perspective of a wide-eyed tourist morphs the ordinary into the extraordinary and reminds you that, for all its challenges, life is still profoundly beautiful.

10

OCTOBER

WE ALL HAVE OUR OWN CHALLENGES

Your hardships may look different than someone else's, but they are not better or worse. If you could experience everyone else's problems for just a few minutes, you'd quickly take yours back. Each of us will experience the grief of loss, the thrill of love, the devastation of not belonging, and the healing of friendship. Others may not experience them in the exact same ways as you do, but their experiences are no less real or powerful than yours. Don't compare your problems to those of others, because we all have our own heavy burdens to carry.

11
OCTOBER

SHARE YOUR TRUTH

Communicate from that place in the center of your heart. Share your truth; you deserve to be heard. Speak honestly, and fearlessly share the dreams, stories, and words that may have been locked away.

12
OCTOBER

HUMOR IS A FORM OF HOPE

The world can be wild and unpredictable, but you can find humor among the heaviness. Though humor will not change what is happening, the ability to seek out lightness is an essential tool for living a positive life.

Finding humor is not the same as denial or pretending that whatever unfortunate situation isn't happening. In fact, it's the opposite. To master the ability to tap into humor, your heart must be wide open, your spirit must be full, and your soul must view the world with perspective and possibility. Humor is simply a form of hope.

13

OCTOBER

THERE IS ALWAYS ENOUGH

Even in a world of over seven billion people, there is enough for everyone: enough money, love, opportunity, and possibility. You are not lacking anything that does not already exist. This doesn't mean that there is not an imbalance of access, but it does mean that it is possible for you to attain whatever it is that you want. Achieving what you hope for—love, money, or success, for example—does not mean you must sacrifice or give up something else. There is enough of everything for everyone. You can have what you want, and so too can others.

COMPARISON TRAP

Comparison is a never-ending trap of negativity. So don't compare yourself to others. For every thing that you *don't* have, someone else has even less. For every thing that you do have, there will also be those who have much more. You can never win at comparison.

Instead of comparing yourself to others, be inspired by them. Use the successes of others to ignite your own possibilities, instead of using them to magnify your own shortcomings.

15
OCTOBER

YOUR BIRTHRIGHT IS HAPPINESS

You deserve happiness, and your happiness will not be born of achievement, money, and material success. Being happy comes from within; it is the lens that you view the world through.

Happiness is the understanding that the world you see every day is a mirror of what you believe to be true. Happiness is a perspective, not simply a feeling that comes from having things of external value.

The very first step toward being happier is believing that you deserve to be happy. Answer these prompts, but without listing your material successes: "I am happy because . . ." "I expect the world to be . . ." Note where your answers are aligned or unaligned with your internal truth.

16
OCTOBER

BEGIN WITH YOU

The courage that it takes to genuinely love other people comes first from loving yourself.

17

OCTOBER

~

LIFE IS MEANT TO BE BOTH MESSY AND MAGICAL

Make mistakes—it means you are actually trying. Walk around with your eyes wide open and your feet firmly rooted. Stumble. Fall. Get back up. Cry when you must, and dance when you are compelled to. Laugh. Feel anger and sadness, but allow room for joy and debauchery, too. Life is both this and that, messy and magical. In finding balance, don't forget to leave space for both.

18

OCTOBER

~

SHINE BRIGHTER

Don't ever be afraid to shine. The sun isn't, and it rises brightly every day. Imagine what owning your light in the same way could do for you.

19
OCTOBER

YOU BELONG HERE

You may find yourself wondering where your place is and who your people are, and you may miss what you've never had. Know that you belong here exactly where you are, as you. There is no other place where you'll belong more, because belonging comes from within you. Belonging is a sense of self-acceptance on the inside. So wherever you are, you belong. Wherever you go, you are home. And no one belongs here more than you do.

20
OCTOBER

CHANGE WHAT AIN'T WORKIN'

If you are unhappy with the cards you've been dealt, buy a new deck and deal yourself new ones.

CHOOSE YOUR OWN DIRECTION

"No person has the right to rain on your dreams."

—MARIAN WRIGHT EDELMAN, *THE MEASURE OF OUR SUCCESS*

Don't let someone tell you that the next step you're taking isn't the right one for you. Don't believe anyone who says that you're dreaming something impossible. Don't allow anyone to talk you out of following your dreams. Only you get to choose what dreams align with your soul.

22
OCTOBER

DISAPPOINTMENT IS THE INEVITABLE RESULT OF EXPECTATIONS

Hope, but don't expect, because when your expectations aren't met or fulfilled, the result is disappointment.

The next time your expectations inevitably lead to disappointment, shift your perception: What if, instead of seeing disappointment as a negative experience, you saw it as a compass directing you to something even better?

23
OCTOBER

LET GO OF NEGATIVITY

Negative feelings, like all bulky things, get so heavy over time that you simply have to let them go. Free yourself of feelings that are weighing you down. If they've become too cumbersome to bear, they've already served whatever purpose they were intended for. So, it is safe for you to set them down and move forward without them.

24
OCTOBER

THE ONLY ONE YOU CAN CHANGE IS YOURSELF

There is deep wisdom in knowing that the only one you can change is yourself. If you find that the world around you isn't what you'd like it to be, consider what you can do to create small changes within yourself.

For example, if you find that everything you read is negative, choose to read something else. If you notice that people around you don't seem happy, give yourself permission to be happier. In doing so, you may notice that your happiness becomes contagious.

What in your life aren't you happy about? What can you change in yourself to create small (or big) changes around you?

25

OCTOBER

BE YOURSELF

By being fully yourself, you give others permission to be themselves around you. And creating a safe space of acceptance, empathy, and kindness—for yourself and others—is a rare human superpower. Be more you, because by doing so, you give others permission to be more them.

26

OCTOBER

CREATE CIRCUMSTANCES

You will fall—yes, you will. But get up. Each time, get back up.

Look for circumstances that align with the life you want to live. If you can't find them, create them. There is no one better suited to construct your dreams than you.

Get to it.

27
OCTOBER

VERY FEW THINGS ARE IMPOSSIBLE

Regardless of the stories you've heard or the cards you've been dealt, you can do anything at all until you tell yourself that it is impossible. It is only with this simple word that your world becomes limited. Your words and your thoughts become your reality, so remind yourself that something is impossible to do only until someone does it.

28
OCTOBER

YOU ARE AS READY AS YOU'LL EVER BE

Go for it. Do the thing you've been dreaming of, thinking about, or pining over. Follow your intuition and not your fears. Stop talking yourself out of whatever you've been hoping for. You are as ready as you'll ever be, and procrastinating won't make you more ready later. Make the leap—now.

29
OCTOBER

YOU WILL GET IT DONE WHEN YOU NEED TO

In those moments when you simply cannot move forward, don't try to.

Surrender what you feel like you should do. Temporarily let it go. Today may not be the day for whatever it is to get done. The world will not come crashing down, and tomorrow will still be a new day with wide-open possibilities.

Forcing yourself to do anything when you are not in the right mind-set will only make the situation more daunting. Walk away, surrender, and when you are ready, come back with a clearer understanding and a more positive perspective.

30
OCTOBER

KINDNESS IS CONTAGIOUS

In a sometimes difficult world, kindness is an act of great courage. Choose to be kind when no one else is looking, but also when everyone is watching. Your kindness teaches others that we all deserve respect and consideration. When one person acts with kindness, those around them feel more altruistic as well. That's the reason kindness is contagious. Your act of kindness is a beacon of hope that spreads. Always choose kindness.

31
OCTOBER

A MANTRA FOR SELF-WORTH

In those times when you feel like the world is walking all over you (because those days will come), show yourself extra kindness and love. Use this mantra as often as needed to remind yourself of how deserving you truly are: "I love and respect myself, and I am deserving of love, respect, and kindness from others."

NOVEMBER

1

NOVEMBER

LIMITING BELIEFS

The only limitations that you have are the ones that you've imposed on yourself.

2

NOVEMBER

SEEK PERSPECTIVE, NOT PERFECTION

Challenges will happen and difficult times will arise, because both the dark and the light are important parts of the human experience. But, when you recognize that moments of difficulty will come to pass and that, mostly, life is quite beautiful in its extremes, you become happier. Nurturing this perspective can help you find the bright side of a tough situation and feel more positive about current or past experiences.

3

NOVEMBER

RESPECT, KINDNESS, AND LOVE

You deserve respect, kindness, and love. You are seen, and you matter. Your experiences are valued and valuable. You exist with purpose, and you are loved.

4

NOVEMBER

DO WHAT YOU NEED TO DO

When you need to let everything go and simply surrender, allow yourself to do that. If you need a good cry, cry. If you are angry, allow yourself to be angry. And when you need to dance it all away, dance. Crying can be transformative, feeling emotions is healing, and dancing refreshes the spirit. Show yourself the grace to do whatever you need to, without judgment or inhibitions.

5

NOVEMBER

CULTIVATE HAPPINESS

Happiness is a conscious choice that lights a fire within and fans that fire outward. It is not something that you acquire from others or discover outside of yourself.

What makes you happy? What makes you feel lighter? What experiences make the time seem to fly by? Do more of these things—often. Seek out experiences that set your soul on fire. Cultivate happiness daily in small ways. A happy life is simply all of those smaller happy moments combined.

ASKING FOR HELP IS A SIGN OF STRENGTH

All of us need help sometimes. Trying to carry the weight of the world on your shoulders will simply keep you anchored in a place of regret, futility, and helplessness.

Learn to ask for help. There is no prize for being the most independent. Asking for what you need is a sign of strength: it demonstrates a willingness to take better care of yourself and those you love by seeking the best possible help. In the same way you'd willingly advocate for others, do the same for yourself.

You are not alone; there is a great big world out there waiting to champion you and help you live your very best life.

7
NOVEMBER

HAVE THE COURAGE TO ASK

You won't get what you don't ask for, but you might get what you do.
So ask. Just ask.

8
NOVEMBER

FOCUS ON POSITIVITY

Choosing to change your focus is a powerful way of transforming a situation. Focusing on the positive doesn't mean that you are denying reality or avoiding what isn't working. It simply allows you to work from a grounded place in order to make the most informed decisions from a less emotional place of clarity.

A shift in perspective changes everything. When you're experiencing difficulties, try shifting your perspective to positivity, and see what happens.

9
NOVEMBER

〜

YOU WILL ALWAYS BE OKAY

Being okay doesn't mean that life will be perfect, nor does it presume that everything will turn out better than before. It simply means that you will eventually make it back to a place of equilibrium, because whatever you are currently experiencing or feeling is temporary; it will pass, as everything does. Even if things turn out differently than you expected, take some solace in knowing that you will always be okay, even if you are different than before.

10
NOVEMBER

〜

A WHOLENESS AFFIRMATION

*"I am not broken, nor have I ever been.
I don't need fixing. I am worthy and
complete exactly as I am."*

ALL EMOTIONS ARE RELEVANT

Joy and positive thinking are powerful tools for living well, but so too are sadness, grief, anger, and fear. The human experience calls for us to feel all of these emotions, rather than picking and choosing the ones that are perceived as better.

Feelings are curative and help us successfully make it through challenging situations by getting to the core of them. Don't avoid the emotions that may not feel as positive. There are moments when the only option is to sit still and feel the full spectrum of human emotions. When those times come, feel those emotions. Allow yourself to feel whatever you do in each moment, knowing that joy and happiness will eventually show up once again.

12

NOVEMBER

EVERYTHING YOU FEEL IS A RESULT OF WHAT YOU THINK

You feel what you feel because you think what you think. So if you don't like how you feel, then change what you are thinking.

   You do have control of your own thinking. When life hands you its worst, consider how you could change your perspective of the situation in order to shift your feelings around it.

13

NOVEMBER

QUIET DOWN

Ease up. Relax. Sit still. Breathe deeply. Surrender inward. Take care of yourself. And then begin again.

14
NOVEMBER

~~~

YOU CANNOT CHANGE THE PAST

You cannot change the past. It is done. Leave it behind you, rather than allowing it to anchor you in place and keep you from moving forward. There is hope in looking forward and freedom in letting go. You deserve to have both.

15
NOVEMBER

~~~

SMILING HELPS

When you least feel like it, smile. Even a tiny one makes a big difference. You are not smiling to pretend to be happy, but instead because it's difficult to be unhappy and smile at the same time. Smiling is simply showing yourself a bit of grace during hard times. It does not mask your feelings, but instead lightens the weight of whatever you're carrying. A smile offers temporary relief; it is a gift that you can give yourself at any moment.

THE POWER OF SELF-RESPECT

"To free us from the expectations of others, to give us back to ourselves— there lies the great, the singular power of self-respect."

—JOAN DIDION, *SLOUCHING TOWARDS BETHLEHEM*

17

NOVEMBER

A LONG OVERDUE THANK YOU

Thank you for being kind. Thank you for being considerate. Thank you for caring about others, even when no one else is watching. Thank you for having empathy. Thank you for being authentic. Thank you for loving and respecting yourself. Thank you for being exactly who you are.

18

NOVEMBER

SUCCESS IS WHATEVER YOU SAY IT IS

Don't get entangled in someone else's definition of what success should be. Create your own narrative; forge your own path. Redefine what success is, and allow it to mean whatever you believe it to be.

What does success look like to you?

19
NOVEMBER

YOU BECOME THE COMPANY YOU KEEP

Surround yourself with people who uplift your spirit and set fire to your soul; they will inspire you to live boldly and thrive. Cultivate an inner circle that embodies whomever you hope to be in the world; they will prepare you to flourish. Walk alongside those who accept others and love wholeheartedly; they will teach you how to be loved unconditionally. To be courageous enough to surround yourself with genuinely kind people is to show that you are genuinely kind as well.

20
NOVEMBER

THE DILEMMA OF TIME

The dilemma with time is that we often think we have more than we do. But today, *right now*—this is all we are guaranteed. Our time is limited, and there is no negotiating that reality. What will you do with the time that you have left?

21
NOVEMBER

~~~

FORGIVENESS IS SELF-COMPASSION

Forgiveness is not an attempt to change what you have experienced, but an act of considerable self-compassion. Withholding forgiveness causes grief and heartache that you don't deserve. When you forgive, you heal, and when you heal, you move forward.

And as you do, you begin again.

22
NOVEMBER

~~~

CHANGING YOUR THOUGHTS

The only way to shift your thoughts is to consciously catch yourself when you think thoughts that don't make you feel good. Do that over and over again, and eventually your thoughts do change. This is a practice, and it will take time. Be patient.

23

NOVEMBER

~~~

WHAT YOU CULTIVATE BECOMES YOUR REALITY

If you focus your attention on hatred, negativity, and sadness, these become your truth. You expect hatred, negativity, and sadness of others and witness them wherever you go. Essentially, you teach your brain to be on heightened alert for these qualities, because they are exactly what you expect.

On the other hand, if you focus on empathy, kindness, and happiness, then these become your reality. You seek empathy, kindness, and happiness in those you surround yourself with and expect to see these qualities in the greater world around you.

What you focus on is exactly what you will see more of, and what you neglect is what will diminish. So which qualities and emotions will you focus on? How will you focus on them? The more specific you can be, the more likely you will cultivate your chosen qualities and emotions with intention.

24
NOVEMBER

~

RELENTLESSLY PURSUE WHAT MATTERS MOST

It is easy to let the outer workings of daily life sidetrack you on the way to your dreams. But stay focused. Remind yourself often of what matters most to you, and relentlessly pursue it.

What pursuits have you let go of because life simply got in the way? How can you reengage with these passions and interests?

25
NOVEMBER

~

YOU ARE NOT FOR EVERYONE

Fitting in is overrated. You are not for everyone; don't strive to be.

26
NOVEMBER

HAPPINESS TAKES COMMITMENT

Happiness takes dedication to not accepting anything less than. Happiness is not a state of euphoria, but rather a state of wellness, peace, and innate love. Don't look outside of yourself for it, because what you will find will only be temporary.

What makes you unhappy? What makes you happy? Commit to asking yourself these questions often.

27
NOVEMBER

A MANTRA FOR HAVING FAITH

"I am loved, I am supported, and I am taken care of even when I don't know how I am."

28
NOVEMBER

SHOW GRATITUDE FOR ALL THINGS

Have gratitude for things large and small, every day. A gratitude practice reminds you how much you have, even alongside all that you perceive to be lacking.

Be grateful that you have a wàrm bed to sleep in, that you are close enough to nature that you can touch and smell grass, that clean water freely flows through your faucet, that you get to spend another day with loved ones, that you can see the world through your eyes, that you wake up each day.

What are you grateful for? How might your mind-set shift if you wrote a daily gratitude list?

29
NOVEMBER

THIS IS SELF-CONFIDENCE

When you believe in yourself, you don't have to convince anyone else of your significance.

30
NOVEMBER

~~~

HOW TO LIVE A GOOD LIFE

With each decision you make, you determine how you will live your life. Here are a few instructions to help you make wise decisions:

Love well.
Hold tight to your dreams.
Fail, fall, try again, then maybe one more time. Eventually,
    you get up.
Stand tall.
Stretch and grow.
Create and play.
Laugh.
Fall again. And again.

Use these instructions as a guide, or don't. Make the conscious choice to live well, whatever that means to you.

DECEMBER

1
DECEMBER

~

AN EXERCISE IN SELF-LOVE

Instead of criticizing who you aren't, what if you spent time focusing on what makes you extraordinary?

Write a list of 25 qualities or physical traits that you absolutely love about yourself. Take as much time as you need, and keep writing until you fill up the list. No judgments allowed. When you are finished, read it one more time and then tuck the list away. Set a reminder to come back to it in six months (or sooner, if you'd prefer).

Repeat this exercise yearly as a part of your birthday celebration, or simply use this as often as you would like. There's no such thing as too much self-love.

2
DECEMBER

~

THE REJECTION MYTH

Rejection is simply someone's opinion. Do not allow it to mean anything more than that.

3
DECEMBER

A MANTRA FOR IMPERMANENCE

"My situation is temporary; nothing is permanent, not even my problems."

4
DECEMBER

GIVE YOUR HEART ROOM TO SPEAK

When you are seeking answers, spending time in silence can often be more powerful than any amount of questioning, searching, or researching. Soften in and let go of the need to constantly move. Go for a walk alone to feel fresh air on your face. Sit quietly with a warm drink in hand. Allow your mind the time it needs to clear. There is space within the silence. When you give your heart the room it needs to speak, it will.

5
DECEMBER

COMPASSION AND SELF-COMPASSION

"If you are continually judging and criticizing yourself while trying to be kind to others, you are drawing artificial boundaries and distinctions that only lead to feelings of separation and isolation."

—KRISTIN NEFF, *SELF-COMPASSION*

You cannot have compassion for others until you first feel compassion for yourself. How do you show self-compassion?

SHAME IS SUFFERING IN SILENCE

You are human. You deserve to be here. You are wanted. You are loved. You are whole.

The only power that shame has over you is the power you grant it. What caused your shame is also the channel for your grit, resilience, and empathy. You are who you've become because of the sum of your experiences, both the good and the bad. Sharing your shame with someone else normalizes who you are (because you are normal) and removes the influence that shame has over you.

Can you share your shame with someone you trust and transform it into a bond of understanding, hope, and empathy? How might you begin to share your truth in the hopes of releasing shame?

7

~

MAKE MISTAKES

Make mistakes often; they will teach you who you are. Be willing to do things wrong in an effort to learn how to do them differently. Mistakes encourage you to grow and make you resilient. They will allow you to become better, stronger, and wiser.

Have perspective. Ask yourself this question: "Will anyone get hurt if this doesn't work out?" If the answer is no, explore what you want to do, and be willing to get it wrong.

Not being afraid to make mistakes will give you a lifetime of adventure and invaluable lessons. Try, fail, try again, dust off, and thrive.

8
DECEMBER

~

TRUST YOURSELF

Listen to the advice of others, but also trust yourself. Your intuition is your inner compass: it will point you in the right direction. Surrender to what your heart knows, even when others disagree. Your instincts are usually accurate when you nurture them.

9
DECEMBER

~

CELEBRATE ALL THE THINGS

Life is short—celebrate everything. The small stuff matters just as much as the big stuff. Celebrate all of it—often.

10
DECEMBER

YOU ARE IMPERFECTLY PERFECT

Accepting your shadows is just as important as accepting your light. You are both this and that—angry and happy, joyful and sad, perfect and imperfect. Accepting all of who you are without judgment and condition may just be the truest form of love you'll ever experience.

What do you think when you look in the mirror? What do you tell yourself about your perceived imperfections? Are you accepting of all of who you are, or do you place conditions on yourself (such as, "When I lose or gain five more pounds, I'll be . . ." or "If only I could change this one thing . . .")? Notice the expectations that you set for yourself and how they make you feel.

11
DECEMBER

A MANTRA FOR HAPPINESS

Happiness is a choice, but it's easy to forget that when life gets in the way. Repeat these simple words to yourself as often as you need to: "Even among the craziness of life, my life is pretty damn sweet. I choose to be happy."

12

DECEMBER

~~~

GIVE IN TO THE MAGIC

Give yourself permission to pay more attention to the birds chirping. Eat the marshmallows out of the cereal box without judging yourself. Look for the rainbows after a storm, and then take a picture of them for posterity. Feel the cool breeze on a hot day, and say thank you. Enjoy a glass of wine in the afternoon.

Savor each solitary moment of this life; they are all you have.

13

DECEMBER

~~~

FORGIVE YOURSELF

You are human. Ease up on yourself—you're doing the best you can. Take a break. Breathe deeply, and forgive yourself for everything.

14
DECEMBER

THE UNDERSTANDING OF LIFE

Life can be messy, unexpected, and complicated, but it can also be filled with magic and overwhelming beauty. You can push up against this contradiction or choose to flow alongside it; the decision is yours. Accepting life as it is allows you the freedom to bend without breaking, regardless of what life sends your way.

15
DECEMBER

THE JOB OF BEING

There will be days when your favorite thing to do is nothing. Allow yourself to do exactly that. Some days *being* is your only job.

16
DECEMBER

PURSUE YOUR OWN BEST LIFE

Do work that you love, regardless of what anyone else thinks. Live in a way that makes you proud. Keep good company. Make space for creativity. Drink good coffee or tea. Smile on the inside. Learn from others. Love well. Dream. Repeat.

17
DECEMBER

CAN I?

Yes. The answer is yes. There is no reason you couldn't. You absolutely can. You could. You should. Go on, do it.

Remember this whenever you are questioning your own capability. The answer is always yes.

THE INNER CRITIC

That voice in your head questioning every decision that you make is your inner critic. Your inner critic is conditioned to be a bully, but you can change how you respond to it.

First, notice when the inner critic shuts down your thoughts and ideas. What is it saying? How do you physically feel when its harsh words arise?

Then, tell yourself the opposite of what your inner critic is telling you, even if you don't quite believe it just yet. For example, if your inner critic says, "You are not experienced enough for this," tell yourself, "I have all the experience I need to begin." Eventually, you will believe your own words instead of your inner critic's. This is a practice that takes time, so be patient with yourself as you learn to counter the negative beliefs that your inner critic is embodying.

You can also write a list of all the negative things that your inner critic tries to get you to believe about yourself. Then, write down what you would say to someone you love if they said these same negative things to themselves. Say those positive things to yourself.

19
DECEMBER

WHAT YOU SEE IS WHAT YOU REFLECT BACK

You see in others what you put out into the world.

When you are vulnerable enough to be your truest self, you find authenticity in others.

When you are jaded and cynical, you see that in others, too, and the world becomes a place filled with distrust.

Each day, you consciously choose who you want to be, and that choice is reflected back to you through the people you meet and how you spend your time. Will you meet love with love, or will you meet cynicism with cynicism? Who will you choose to be?

20
DECEMBER

BEAUTY LIES WITHIN IMPERFECTION

Your perceived imperfections are the source of your beauty. Love yourself exactly as you are, and so, too, will others.

21

DECEMBER

THE VALUE OF CONTRAST

Life is both the dark and the light. There will be days that you wish never happened, but there will be other days so perfect that they bring you to your knees with astonishment. The only way out of the difficult times is to go through them, and the only way to experience the good times is to rise up alongside them. This is life. Get through and rise up. Get through and rise up. In getting through, we learn resilience, and in rising up, we learn to flourish and soar.

22
DECEMBER

BECOME A PERMISSION GIVER FOR OTHERS

Empower folks to shine more brightly. Be kind, especially when it's most difficult. Believe in humanity. Show compassion. Demonstrate empathy. Forgive others.

Doing these things won't always be easy. But in practicing these acts of humility, you awaken possibility in others and become a permission-giver for divine change.

23
DECEMBER

WHO WERE YOU ONCE?

Who were you before you began becoming the person others
told you to be?

Where did you go?
What were you like?
What did you enjoy?

Who were you when you trusted and actually listened to your
truest self?

24
DECEMBER

~~

YOU OWE IT TO YOURSELF...

To stand up for what you know and have a real opinion,
    even if others disagree.
To accept all of who you are, in a mash-up of your full glory.
To be as compassionate to yourself as you are to others.
To show up for yourself even when others don't.
To be brave in the face of ignorance.
To stand up and empower others.
To trust yourself enough to know that you are exactly where you
    should be (even if where you are ain't pretty in this moment).
To be willing to be wrong and to listen to the opinions of others.
And, finally, to know that for every loss, there will be a win.
So brace yourself for the beauty that is right in front of you.
    You are magic, and you owe it to yourself to know that, too.

FEARLESSNESS IS OVERRATED

Being fearless is overrated. Fear is a guide: get used to it, and it will teach you things.

Get comfortable being uncomfortable. Be curious, and allow yourself to be vulnerable in the face of fear. Use fear as a way of knowing that you are knee-deep in greatness. Do not run the other way.

And do not seek fearlessness. If you do, you run the risk of chasing it forever and never doing the work that you were put on this great big planet to do.

26
DECEMBER

HOLD TIGHT TO FRIENDSHIPS

Hold tightly to your friends. They are the memory keepers of your life. They are your light, your happiness, and your eyes when the world darkens (or shines too brightly) around you. They lift you up when you cannot stand, and they run alongside you when you are moving too fast. They will show you the way and tell you the truth. In a sometimes crazy world, they are your compass and a beacon of love.

27
DECEMBER

BE NICE

The world is hard, and we are all more delicate than we seem. Be nicer than you think you should be.

28
DECEMBER

~

WHEN YOU CANNOT CHANGE WHAT IS

At the core of love is the pure acceptance of what is. There is deep wisdom in allowing yourself to simply bear witness to what is without needing to change it. You cannot change the unchangeable, regardless of how deep your desire to may be. In these moments, acceptance is the greatest gift you can give yourself.

29
DECEMBER

~

SAY THANK YOU

Instead of loathing what can not be changed, say thank you. Yes, thank you.

"Thank you for giving me no more than I can handle."

"Thank you for this experience that I know will have valuable lessons for me."

"Thank you for giving me an opportunity to grow."

Notice how this shift in mind-set changes your experience.

30
DECEMBER

~~~

IF IT MAKES YOU HAPPY, DO IT

Don't overthink it. Whether it is a big leap or a tiny step, if it makes you happy, it's taking you in the right direction. So do it.

31
DECEMBER

~~~

HOW WILL YOU SPEND YOUR LIFE?

Graciously let go of what didn't serve you, and open up to the possibilities that are yet to come.

Reflect on the past as you move forward. What have you done in the past year? What did the past year teach you about yourself? Which experiences shifted who you are? How will you evolve next year?

Choose three words for the new year that will represent the path you hope to take.

Further Reading

Brown, Brené. *Braving the Wilderness: The Quest for True Belonging and the Courage to Stand Alone*. New York: Random House, 2017.

Cameron, Julia. *The Artist's Way: A Spiritual Path to Higher Creativity*. New York: Jeremy P. Tarcher, 1992.

Chodron, Pema. *When Things Fall Apart: Heart Advice for Difficult Times*. Twentieth anniversary edition. Boulder, CO: Shambhala, 2016.

Dyer, Wayne. *The Power of Intention: Learning to Co-Create Your World Your Way*. Carlsbad, CA: Hay House, 2005.

Fredrickson, Barbara. *Positivity: Top-Notch Research Reveals the 3-to-1 Ratio That Will Change Your Life*. New York: Three Rivers Press, 2009.

Kabat-Zinn, Jon. *Wherever You Go, There You Are: Mindfulness Meditation in Everyday Life*. Tenth anniversary edition. New York: Hachette/Hyperion, 2005.

Pressfield, Steven. *The War of Art: Break Through the Blocks and Win Your Inner Creative Battles*. New York: Black Irish Entertainment, 2002.

Salzberg, Sharon. *The Force of Kindness: Change Your Life with Love and Compassion*. Boulder, CO: Sounds True, 2010.

Seligman, Martin. *Flourish: A Visionary New Understanding of Health and Well-being*. New York: Free Press, 2012.

About the Author

CYNDIE SPIEGEL is an outspoken speaker (who sometimes drops the F-bomb casually and also uses words like "manifesting" and "belonging"), community builder (she builds the diverse communities that she couldn't find out in the wild), and all-around executive truth-teller on a mission to empower others to live more boldly, refine their mind-sets for good, and help them realize their most ridiculously inspired dreams.

Her unique and relatable blend of straight talk, sass, and powerful inspiration has made her a sought-after workshop facilitator and keynote speaker.

Cyndie is a yogi, thought-provoker, former fashion industry veteran, and adjunct professor.

She lives in Brooklyn, NY, with her photographer husband and two overly particular cats.

Find more about Cyndie:
CyndieSpiegel.com
Instagram: @CyndieSpiegel